THE YALE SHAKESPEARE

Revised Edition

General Editors

Helge Kökeritz and Charles T. Prouty

Published on the fund

given to the Yale University Press in 1917

by the members of the

Kingsley Trust Association

(Scroll and Key Society of Yale College)

to commemorate the seventy-fifth anniversary

of the founding of the society

THE TRAGEDY OF
TROILUS AND CRESSIDA

Edited by Jackson J. Campbell

LUX ET VERITAS

NEW HAVEN : YALE UNIVERSITY PRESS

London: Geoffrey Cumberlege, Oxford University Press

FIRST PUBLISHED, JUNE, 1927
REVISED EDITION, MARCH, 1956

Preface of the General Editors

AS the late Professor Tucker Brooke has observed, practically all modern editions of Shakespeare are 18th-century versions of the plays, based on the additions, alterations, and emendations of editors of that period. It has been our purpose, as it was Professor Brooke's, to give the modern reader Shakespeare's plays in the approximate form of their original appearance.

About half the plays appeared in quarto form before the publication of the First Folio in 1623. Thus for a large number of plays the only available text is that of the Folio. In the case of quarto plays our policy has been to use that text as the basis of the edition, unless it is clear that the text has been contaminated.

Interesting for us today is the fact that there are no act or scene divisions in the Quartos with the exception of *Othello*, which does mark Acts I, II, IV, and V but lacks indications of scenes. Even in the Folio, although act divisions are generally noted, only a part of the scenes are divided. In no case, either in Quarto or Folio, is there any indication of the place of action. The manifold scene divisions for the battle in such a play as *Antony and Cleopatra*, together with such locations as "Another part of the field," are the additions of the 18th century.

We have eliminated all indications of the place and time of action, because there is no authority for them in the originals and because Shakespeare gives such information, when it is requisite for understanding the play, through the dialogue of the actors. We have been sparing in our use of added scene and, in some cases, act divisions, because these frequently impede the flow of the action, which in Shakespeare's time was curiously like that of modern films.

Spelling has been modernized except when the original clearly indicates a pronunciation unlike our own, e.g. *desart* (desert), *divel* (devil), *banket* (banquet), and often in such Elizabethan syncopations as *ere* (e'er), *stolne* (stol'n), and *tane* (ta'en). In reproducing such forms we have followed the inconsistent usage of the original.

We have also preserved much more of the original capitalization than is usual, for often this is a part of the meaning. In like manner we have tended to adopt the lineation of the original in many cases where modern editors print prose as verse or verse as prose. We have, moreover, followed the original punctuation wherever it was practicable.

In verse we print a final *-ed* to indicate its full syllabic value, otherwise *'d*. In prose we have followed the inconsistencies of the original in this respect.

Our general practice has been to include in footnotes all information a reader needs for immediate understanding of the given page. In somewhat empiric fashion we repeat glosses as we think the reader needs to be reminded of the meaning. Further information is given in notes (indicated by the letter *N* in the footnotes) to be found at the back of each volume. Appendices deal with the text and sources of the play.

Square brackets indicate material not found in the original text. Long emendations or lines taken from another authoritative text of a play are indicated in the footnotes for the information of the reader. We have silently corrected obvious typographical errors.

vi

CONTENTS

[THE ACTORS' NAMES

PRIAM, *King of Troy*
HECTOR
TROILUS
PARIS   } *his sons*
DEIPHOBUS
HELENUS
AENEAS   } *Trojan commanders*
ANTENOR
CALCHAS, *a Trojan priest, taking part with the Greeks*
PANDARUS, *uncle to Cressida*
AGAMEMNON, *the Grecian general*
MENELAUS, *his brother*
ACHILLES
AJAX
ULYSSES   } *Grecian commanders*
NESTOR
DIOMEDES
PATROCLUS
THERSITES, *a deformed and scurrilous Grecian*
ALEXANDER, *servant to Cressida*
Servant to Troilus, Servant to Paris, Servant to Diomedes

HELEN, *wife to Menelaus*
ANDROMACHE, *wife to Hector*
CASSANDRA, *daughter to Priam; a prophetess*
CRESSIDA, *daughter to Calchas*

Trojan and Greek Soldiers, and attendants.]

THE TRAGEDY OF
TROILUS AND CRESSIDA

The Prologue

In Troy there lies the scene. From isles of Greece
The princes orgillous, their high blood chaf'd,
Have to the port of Athens sent their ships
Fraught with the ministers and instruments
Of cruel war. Sixty-and-nine that wore   5
Their crownets regal, from th' Athenian bay
Put forth toward Phrygia and their vow is made
To ransack Troy, within whose strong immures
The ravish'd Helen, Menelaus' queen,   9
With wanton Paris sleeps, and that's the quarrel.
To Tenedos they come,
And the deep-drawing [barks] do there disgorge
Their warlike fraughtage. Now on Dardan plains
The fresh and yet unbruised Greeks do pitch
Their brave pavilions. Priam's six-gated city,   15
Dardan and Timbria, Helias, Chetas, Troien,
And Antenonidus, with massy staples
And corresponsive and fulfilling bolts
[Sperr] up the sons of Troy.
Now expectation, tickling skittish spirits,   20

---

2 **orgillous** orgulous, proud. 8 **immures** walls. 12 **barks** F *barke*. (F refers throughout to the First Folio of 1623.) 13 **Dardan** the plains around Troy. 15 **brave** splendid. 17 **Antenonidus** N. (N refers throughout to the corresponding note given at the end of the text.) 18 **fulfilling** which fill their sockets completely. 19 **Sperr up** pen up, enclose; F *Stirre vp* N.

On one and other side, Troyan and Greek,
Sets all on hazard. And hither am I come,
A prologue arm'd, but not in confidence
Of author's pen, or actor's voice, but suited
In like conditions as our argument,   25
To tell you, fair beholders, that our play
Leaps ore the vaunt and firstlings of those broils,
Beginning in the middle, starting thence away
To what may be digested in a play.
Like, or find fault; do as your pleasures are: 30
Now good or bad, 'tis but the chance of war.

22 **hazard** chance. 23–5 **prologue arm'd . . . argument** N. 25
argument plot, story. 27 **ore** o'er, over. **vaunt** van, beginning.

Act I

SCENE 1

Enter Pandarus and Troilus.

Troilus. Call here my varlet; I'll unarm again.
Why should I war without the walls of Troy
That find such cruel battle here within?
Each Troyan that is master of his heart,
Let him to field; Troilus, alas, hath none.   5
    Pandarus. Will this gear nere be mended?
    Troilus. The Greeks are strong, and skillful to their
        strength,
Fierce to their skill, and to their fierceness valiant;
But I am weaker than a woman's tear,
Tamer than sleep, fonder than ignorance,   10
Less valiant than the virgin in the night,
And skilless as unpractic'd infancy.
    Pandarus. Well, I have told you enough of this.
For my part, I'll not meddle nor make no farther.
He that will have a cake out of the wheat must needs
tarry the grinding.   16
    Troilus. Have I not tarried?
    Pandarus. Ay, the grinding; but you must tarry
the bolting.
    Troilus. Have I not tarried?   20
    Pandarus. Ay, the bolting; but you must tarry the
[leavening].

---

1 **varlet** servant. 6 **gear** matter, affair. **nere** ne'er, never. 7 **to** in
addition to. 10 **fonder** more foolish. 19 **bolting** sifting. 22 **leavening** F *leau'ing.*

Troilus. Still have I tarried.

Pandarus. Ay, to the leavening; but here's yet in the word hereafter: the kneading, the making of the cake, the heating of the oven, and the baking. Nay, you must stay the cooling, too, or you may chance to burn your lips. 28

Troilus. Patience herself, what goddess ere she be, Doth lesser blench at sufferance than I do.
At Priam's royal table do I sit,
And when fair Cressid comes into my thoughts—
So, traitor, then she comes, when she is thence.

Pandarus. Well, she look'd yesternight fairer than ever I saw her look, or any woman else. 35

Troilus. I was about to tell thee: when my heart, As wedged with a sigh, would rive in twain
Lest Hector or my father should perceive me,
I have (as when the sun doth light ascorn)
Buried this sigh in wrinkle of a smile; 40
But sorrow, that is couch'd in seeming gladness,
Is like that mirth fate turns to sudden sadness.

Pandarus. And her hair were not somewhat darker than Helen's—well, go to—there were no more comparison between the women. But for my part, she is my kinswoman; I would not, as they term it, praise her, but I would somebody had heard her talk yesterday as I did. I will not dispraise your sister Cassandra's wit, but—

Troilus. O Pandarus! I tell thee Pandarus— 50
When I do tell thee, 'There my hopes lie drown'd,'
Reply not in how many fadoms deep

24–5 here's . . . hereafter N. 30 blench flinch. 33 So . . . thence N. 39 ascorn in mockery. 43 And and if N. 44 go to never mind. were would be. 47 her F *it.* 52 fadoms fathoms.

They lie indrench'd. I tell thee, 'I am mad
In Cressid's love.' Thou answer'st, 'She is fair,'
Pour'st in the open ulcer of my heart   55
Her eyes, her hair, her cheek, her gait, her voice;
Handlest in thy discourse, O, that her hand,
In whose comparison all whites are ink,
Writing their own reproach, to whose soft seizure
The cygnet's down is harsh, and spirit of sense   60
Hard as the palm of ploughman. This thou tell'st
      me,
As true thou tell'st me, when I say I love her.
But saying thus, instead of oil and balm
Thou lay'st in every gash that love hath given me
The knife that made it.   65

  Pandarus. I speak no more than truth.

  Troilus. Thou dost not speak so much.

  Pandarus. Faith, I'll not meddle in't. Let her be as
she is. If she be fair, 'tis the better for her; and she
be not, she has the mends in her own hands.   70

  Troilus. Good Pandarus! How now, Pandarus?

  Pandarus. I have had my labor for my travel, ill
thought on of her and ill thought on of you; gone
between and between, but small thanks for my labor.

  Troilus. What, art thou angry, Pandarus? What,
with me?   76

  Pandarus. Because she's kin to me, therefore she's
not so fair as Helen. And she were not kin to me, she
would be as fair on Friday as Helen is on Sunday.
But what care I? I care not and she were a black-a-
moor; 'tis all one to me.   81

  Troilus. Say I she is not fair?

59 seizure grasp. 60 spirit of sense N. 70 mends remedy. 72 travel
travail, pains. 73 thought on of thought of by. 79 fair . . .
Sunday N.

Pandarus. I do not care whether you do or no. She's a fool to stay behind her father. Let her to the Greeks, and so I'll tell her the next time I see her. For my part, I'll meddle nor make no more i' th' matter.   87

Troilus. Pandarus?

Pandarus. Not I.

Troilus. Sweet Pandarus.   90

Pandarus. Pray you, speak no more to me. I will leave all as I found it, and there an end.

Exit Pandarus.

Sound alarum.

Troilus. Peace, you ungracious clamors! Peace, rude sounds!

Fools on both sides! Helen must needs be fair,
When with your blood you daily paint her thus.   95
I cannot fight upon this argument;
It is too starv'd a subject for my sword.
But Pandarus—O gods! how do you plague me!
I cannot come to Cressid but by Pandar,
And he's as tetchy to be woo'd to woo   100
As she is stubborn-chaste against all suit.
Tell me, Apollo, for thy Daphne's love,
What Cressid is, what Pandar, and what we.
Her bed is India; there she lies, a pearl;
Between our Ilium and where she resides   105
Let it be call'd the wild and wand'ring flood,
Ourself the merchant, and this sailing Pandar
Our doubtful hope, our convoy and our bark.

Alarum. Enter Aeneas.

84 father N. 100 tetchy peevish. 105 Ilium N.

Aeneas. How now, Prince Troilus? Wherefore not afield?

Troilus. Because not there. This woman's answer sorts,   110

For womanish it is to be from thence.

What news, Aeneas, from the field today?

Aeneas. That Paris is returned home, and hurt.

Troilus. By whom, Aeneas?

Aeneas.   Troilus, by Menelaus.

Troilus. Let Paris bleed! 'Tis but a scar to scorn.

Paris is gor'd with Menelaus' horn.   *Alarum.*

Aeneas. Hark, what good sport is out of town today!   117

Troilus. Better at home, if 'would I might' were 'may.'

But to the sport abroad, are you bound thither?

Aeneas. In all swift haste.

Troilus.   Come, go we then togither.

Exeunt.

SCENE 2

Enter Cressid and her Man.

Cressida. Who were those went by?

Man.   Queen Hecuba and Helen.

Cressida. And whether go they?

Man.   Up to the eastern tower,

Whose height commands as subject all the vale,

To see the battle. Hector, whose patience

110 **sorts** is fitting. 114 **to scorn** to be scorned. 115 **horn** N. 122 **togither** N. 1 those went those who went. 2 **whether** whither.

Is as a virtue fix'd, today was mov'd.   5
He chides Andromache and strooke his armorer,
And, like as there were husbandry in war,
Before the sun rose he was harness'd light
And to the field goes he, where every flower
Did as a prophet weep what it foresaw   10
In Hector's wrath.

   Cressida.   What was his cause of anger?

   Man. The noise goes, this: there is among the
       Greeks
A lord of Troyan blood, nephew to Hector;
They call him Ajax.

   Cressida.   Good, and what of him?

   Man. They say he is a very man *per se*   15
And stands alone.

   Cressida. So do all men, unless they are drunk, sick,
or have no legs.   18

   Man. This man, lady, hath robb'd many beasts of
their particular additions. He is as valiant as the
lion, churlish as the bear, slow as the elephant; a
man into whom nature hath so crowded humors that
his valor is crush'd into folly, his folly sauced with
discretion. There is no man hath a virtue that he
hath not a glimpse of, nor any man an attaint but
he carries some stain of it. He is melancholy without
cause and merry against the hair. He hath the joints
of everything, but everything so out of joint that he

is a gouty Briareus, many hands and no use; or pur-
blinded Argus, all eyes and no sight.   30

Cressida. But how should this man, that makes me
smile, make Hector angry?

Man. They say he yesterday cop'd Hector in the
battle and stroke him down, the disdain and shame
whereof hath ever since kept Hector fasting and
waking.   36

Enter Pandarus.

Cressida. Who comes here?

Man. Madam, your uncle Pandarus.

Cressida. Hector's a gallant man.

Man. As may be in the world, lady.   40

Pandarus. What's that? What's that?

Cressida. Good morrow, uncle Pandarus.

Pandarus. Good morrow, cousin Cressid. What do
you talk of? Good morrow, Alexander. How do you,
cousin? When were you at Ilium?   45

Cressida. This morning, uncle.

Pandarus. What were you talking of when I came?
Was Hector arm'd and gone ere you came to Ilium?
Helen was not up, was she?   49

Cressida. Hector was gone but Helen was not up.

Pandarus. E'en so. Hector was stirring early.

Cressida. That were we talking of, and of his anger.

Pandarus. Was he angry?

Cressida. So he says here.   54

Pandarus. True, he was so. I know the cause too.
He'll lay about him today, I can tell them that. And

29 **Briareus** a monster in Greek mythology who had a hundred
hands and fifty heads. 30 **Argus** a giant in Greek mythology who
had a hundred eyes. 31 **should** could. 33 **cop'd** fought. 34 **stroke**
struck. 43 **cousin** N.

there's Troilus will not come far behind him; let them take heed of Troilus. I can tell them that too.

Cressida. What, is he angry too?   59

Pandarus. Who, Troilus? Troilus is the better man of the two.

Cressida. O Jupiter! There's no comparison.

Pandarus. What, not between Troilus and Hector? Do you know a man if you see him?   64

Cressida. Ay, if I ever saw him before and knew him.

Pandarus. Well, I say Troilus is Troilus.

Cressida. Then you say as I say, for I am sure he is not Hector.   69

Pandarus. No, [nor] Hector is not Troilus in some degrees.

Cressida. 'Tis just to each of them. He is himself.

Pandarus. Himself? Alas, poor Troilus, I would he were.

Cressida. So he is.   75

Pandarus. Condition I had gone barefoot to India.

Cressida. He is not Hector.

Pandarus. Himself? No, he's not himself; would a were himself. Well, the gods are above; time must friend or end. Well, Troilus, well. I would my heart were in her body! No, Hector is not a better man than Troilus.   82

Cressida. Excuse me.

Pandarus. He is elder.

Cressida. Pardon me, pardon me.   85

Pandarus. Th' other's not come to't. You shall tell me another tale when th' other's come to't. Hector shall not have his will this year.

70 **nor** F *not.* 76 **Condition** on condition that N. 78 **a** he N.
79–80 **time . . . end** N. 80 **heart** feelings. 88 **will** N.

Cressida. He shall not need it, if he have his own.

Pandarus. Nor his qualities. 90

Cressida. No matter.

Pandarus. Nor his beauty.

Cressida. 'Twould not become him; his own's better.

Pandarus. You have no judgment, niece. Helen herself swore th' other day that Troilus for a brown favor, for so 'tis, I must confess—not brown neither— 97

Cressida. No, but brown.

Pandarus. Faith, to say truth, brown and not brown. 100

Cressida. To say the truth, true and not true.

Pandarus. She prais'd his complexion above Paris.

Cressida. Why, Paris hath color enough.

Pandarus. So he has. 104

Cressida. Then Troilus should have too much, if she prais'd him above; his complexion is higher than his. He having color enough, and the other higher, is too flaming a praise for a good complexion. I had as lieve Helen's golden tongue had commended Troilus for a copper nose. 110

Pandarus. I swear to you I think Helen loves him better than Paris.

Cressida. Then she's a merry Greek indeed!

Pandarus. Nay, I am sure she does. She came to him th' other day into the compass'd window—and you know he has not past three or four hairs on his chin— 117

95–96 **brown favor** dark complexion. 105 **should** would. 106 **higher** more vivid, colorful. 109 **lieve** lief. 113 **merry Greek** a gay, lively person (slang). 115 **compass'd window** bay window.

Cressida. Indeed, a tapster's arithmetic may soon bring his particulars therein to a total.

Pandarus. Why, he is very young, and yet will he within three pound lift as much as his brother Hector. 122

Cressida. Is he so young a man, and so old a lifter?

Pandarus. But to prove to you that Helen loves him: she came and puts me her white hand to his cloven chin— 126

Cressida. Juno have mercy! How came it cloven?

Pandarus. Why, you know 'tis dimpled. I think his smiling becomes him better than any man in all Phrygia. 130

Cressida. O, he smiles valiantly.

Pandarus. Does he not?

Cressida. O yes, and 'twere a cloud in autumn.

Pandarus. Why, go to then. But to prove to you that Helen loves Troilus— 135

Cressida. Troilus will stand to the proof, if you'll prove it so.

Pandarus. Troilus? Why, he esteems her no more than I esteem an addle egg. 139

Cressida. If you love an addle egg as well as you love an idle head, you would eat chickens i' th' shell.

Pandarus. I cannot choose but laugh to think how she tickled his chin. Indeed she has a marvel's white hand, I must needs confess.

Cressida. Without the rack. 145

Pandarus. And she takes upon her to spy a white hair on his chin.

118 **tapster's arithmetic** N. 123 **lifter** with a pun on 'shoplifter.' 125 **puts me** puts (*me*, so-called ethical dative, superfluous in modern usage). 139 **addle egg** rotten egg. 143 **marvel's** marvelous. 145 **Without the rack** without being tortured.

Cressida. Alas, poor chin! Many a wart is richer.

Pandarus. But there was such laughing. Queen Hecuba laugh'd that her eyes ran ore.   150

Cressida. With millstones.

Pandarus. And Cassandra laugh'd.

Cressida. But there was more temperate fire under the pot of her eyes. Did her eyes run ore too?

Pandarus. And Hector laugh'd.   155

Cressida. At what was all this laughing?

Pandarus. Marry, at the white hair that Helen spied on Troilus' chin.

Cressida. And't had been a green hair, I should have laugh'd too.   160

Pandarus. They laugh'd not so much at the hair, as at his pretty answer.

Cressida. What was his answer?

Pandarus. Quoth she, 'Here's but two and fifty hairs on your chin, and one of them is white.'   165

Cressida. This is her question.

Pandarus. That's true; make no question of that. 'Two and fifty hairs,' quoth he, 'and one white. That white hair is my father, and all the rest are his sons.' 'Jupiter!' quoth she, 'which of these hairs is Paris, my husband?' 'The forked one,' quoth he. 'Pluck't out and give it him.' But there was such laughing, and Helen so blush'd, and Paris so chaf'd, and all the rest so laugh'd, that it pass'd!   174

Cressida. So let it now, for it has been a great while going by.

151 **With millstones** a proverbial expression, indicating no tears at all. 157 **Marry** a mild oath, having reference to the Virgin Mary. 159 **And't** if it; I.1.43. N. 162 **pretty** clever, apt. 171 **forked** 'horned,' perhaps with the usual reference to cuckold's horns. 174 **pass'd** exceeded all bounds.

Pandarus. Well, cousin, I told you a thing yesterday. Think on't.

Cressida. So I do.   179

Pandarus. I'll be sworn 'tis true. He will weep you
an 'twere a man born in April.   *Sound a retreat.*

Cressida. And I'll spring up in his tears an 'twere
a nettle against May.   183

Pandarus. Hark! They are coming from the field.
Shall we stand up here and see them as they pass
toward Ilium? Good niece, do, sweet niece Cressida.

Cressida. At your pleasure.   187

Pandarus. Here, here, here's an excellent place.
Here we may see most bravely. I'll tell you them all
by their names as they pass by, but mark Troilus
above the rest.   191

Enter Aeneas [and passes over the stage].

Cressida. Speak not so loud.

Pandarus. That's Aeneas. Is not that a brave man?
He's one of the flowers of Troy, I can [tell] you. But
mark Troilus; you shall see anon.   195

Cressida. Who's that?

Enter Antenor [and passes over the stage].

Pandarus. That's Antenor. He has a shrowd wit, I
can tell you, and he's a man good enough. He's one
o' th' soundest judgment in Troy whosoever, and a
proper man of person. When comes Troilus? I'll
show you Troilus anon. If he see me, you shall see
him nod at me.   202

---

183 **against** in expectation of. 189 **bravely** excellently. 194 **tell** F
omits. 197 **shrowd** shrewd. 199 **whosoever** no matter who. 200
proper man of person man of attractive appearance.

14

Cressida. Will he give you the nod?
Pandarus. You shall see.
Cressida. If he do, the rich shall have more.   205

Enter Hector [and passes over the stage].

Pandarus. That's Hector, that, that, look you, that! There's a fellow! Go thy way, Hector. There's a brave man, niece. O brave Hector! Look how he looks. There's a countenance! Is't not a brave man?
Cressida. O brave man!   210
Pandarus. Is a not? It does a man's heart good. Look you what hacks are on his helmet; look you yonder. Do you see? Look you there. There's no jesting; [there's] laying on, tak't off who will, as they say. There be hacks!   215
Cressida. Be those with swords?

Enter Paris [and passes over the stage].

Pandarus. Swords, anything, he cares not. And the divel come to him, it's all one. By God's lid, it does one's heart good. Yonder comes Paris, yonder comes Paris! Look ye yonder, niece. Is't not a gallant man too, is't not? Why, this is brave now. Who said he came hurt home today? He's not hurt. Why, this will do Helen's heart good now, ha? Would I could see Troilus now. You shall [see] Troilus anon.
Cressida. Who's that?   225

Enter Hellenus [and passes over the stage].

203 nod N. 208 brave N. 211 Is a not? Is he not? 214 there's laying on real fighting; F *laying on.* 214 tak't off depreciate it. 215 be are. 218 divel 'devil,' so spelled consistently throughout this play. 218 God's lid 'by God's eyelid,' a mild oath. 224 shall see F *shall.*

Pandarus. That's Hellenus. I marvel where Troilus is. That's Hellenus. I think he went not forth today. That's Hellenus.

Cressida. Can Hellenus fight, uncle?   229

Pandarus. Hellenus? No. Yes, he'll fight indifferent well. I marvel where Troilus is. Hark, do you not hear the people cry 'Troilus'? Hellenus is a priest.

Cressida. What sneaking fellow comes yonder?   233

Enter Troilus [and passes over the stage].

Pandarus. Where? Yonder? That's Deiphobus. 'Tis Troilus! There's a man, niece! Hem? Brave Troilus, the prince of chivalry!

Cressida. Peace, for shame, peace!   237

Pandarus. Mark him, [note] him. O brave Troilus! Look well upon him, niece. Look you how his sword is bloodied, and his helm more hack'd than Hector's. And how he looks, and how he goes. O admirable youth! He nere saw three-and-twenty. Go thy way, Troilus, go thy way. Had I a sister were a Grace or a daughter a goddess, he should take his choice. O admirable man! Paris? Paris is dirt to him, and I warrant, Helen, to change, would give money to boot.   247

Enter common soldiers [and pass over the stage].

Cressida. Here come more.

Pandarus. Asses, fools, dolts! Chaff and bran, chaff and bran. Porredge after meat. I could live and die i' th' eyes of Troilus. Nere look, nere look; the eagles are gone! Crows and daws, crows and daws.

226 marvel wonder. 230 **indifferent** middlingly. 238 note F *not.* 242 nere never. 250 **Porredge** porridge. 251 i' th' eyes of Troilus in Troilus' company.

16

I had rather be such a man as Troilus than Agamemnon and all Greece.   254

Cressida. There is among the Greeks Achilles, a
better man than Troilus.

Pandarus. Achilles? A drayman, a porter, a very
camel.

Cressida. Well, well.   259

Pandarus. Well, well? Why, have you any discretion? Have you any eyes? Do you know what a man
is? Is not birth, beauty, good shape, discourse, manhood, learning, gentleness, virtue, youth, liberality,
and so forth, the spice and salt that seasons a man?

Cressida. Ay, a minc'd man. And then to be bak'd
with no date in the pie, for then the man's date's out.

Pandarus. You are such another woman, one knows
not at what ward you lie.   268

Cressida. Upon my back, to defend my belly; upon
my wit, to defend my wiles; upon my secrecy, to defend mine honesty; my mask, to defend my beauty;
and you to defend all these; and at all these wards
I lie, at a thousand watches.   273

Pandarus. Say one of your watches.   274

Cressida. Nay, I'll watch you for that; and that's
one of the chiefest of them too. If I cannot ward
what I would not have hit, I can watch you for telling how I took the blow, unless it swell past hiding,
and then it's past watching.

Enter Boy.

Pandarus. You are such another!   280

266 **date's out** N. 267 **such another woman** such a perverse
woman. 268 **ward** a defensive posture in fencing. 271 **mask** N.
273 **lie** F has a superfluous *at* after *lie.* 275 **watch** N. 278 **swell
past hiding** a reference to pregnancy.

Boy. Sir. my lord would instantly speak with you.
Pandarus. Where?
Boy. At your own house.
Pandarus. Good, boy, tell him I come. I doubt he be
hurt. Fare ye well, good niece.   [*Exit Boy.*]
Cressida. Adieu, uncle.   286
Pandarus. I'll be with you, niece, by and by.
Cressida. To bring, uncle.
Pandarus. Ay, a token from Troilus.
Cressida. By the same token, you are a bawd.   290
                                Exit Pandarus.
Words, vows, gifts, tears, and love's full sacrifice
He offers in another's enterprise.
But more in Troilus thousandfold I see
Than in the glass of Pandar's praise may be;   294
Yet hold I off. Women are angels wooing;
Things won are done; joy's soul lies in the doing.
That she belov'd knows nought that knows not this:
Men prize the thing ungain'd more than it is.
That she was never yet that ever knew
Love got so sweet as when desire did sue.   300
Therefore this maxim out of love I teach:
'Achievement is command; ungain'd beseech.'
[Then] though my heart's contents firm love doth
      bear,
Nothing of that shall from mine eyes appear.
                                                      Exit.

284 **doubt** respect, fear. 288 **To bring** N. 294 **glass** mirror. 295
wooing when being wooed. 297 **she** woman. 300 **Love got** love
already achieved. 302 **Achievement . . . beseech** N. **beseech**
entreaty. 303 **Then** F *That.*

18

SCENE 3

Sennet. Enter Agamemnon, Nestor, Ulysses, Diomedes, Menelaus, with others.

Agamemnon. Princes,
What grief hath set the jaundice on your cheeks?
The ample proposition that hope makes
In all designs begun on earth below   4
Fails in the promised largeness. Checks and disasters
Grow in the veins of actions highest rear'd;
As knots, by the conflux of meeting sap,
Infect the sound pine and diverts his grain,
Tortive and errant, from his course of growth.
Nor, princes, is it matter new to us   10
That we come short of our suppose so far
That after seven years' siege yet Troy walls stand.
Sith every action that hath gone before
Whereof we have record, trial did draw
Bias and thwart, not answering the aim,   15
And that unbodied figure of the thought
That gave't surmised shape. Why then, you princes,
Do you with cheeks abash'd behold our works
And think them shame, which are indeed nought else
But the protractive trials of great love   20
To find persistive constancy in men?
The fineness of which metal is not found
In Fortune's love; for then the bold and coward,

3 proposition offer. 7 conflux stressed — ′. 8 diverts N. 9
Tortive distorted, twisted. 11 suppose expectation. 13 Sith since.
14 trial the testing by experience, the actual events. 15 Bias
lopsided, not quite perfect N. 20 protractive protracted, drawn
out. 21 persistive persistent. 23 Fortune's N.

The wise and fool, the artist and unread,
The hard and soft, seem all affin'd and kin. 25
But in the wind and tempest of her frown
Distinction with a loud and powerful fan,
Puffing at all, winnows the light away,
And what hath mass or matter by itself
Lies rich in virtue and unmingled. 30
  Nestor. With due observance of thy godly seat,
Great Agamemnon, Nestor shall apply
Thy latest words. In the reproof of chance
Lies the true proof of men. The sea being smooth,
How many shallow bauble boats dare sail 35
Upon her patient breast, making their way
With those of nobler bulk!
But let the ruffian Boreas once enrage
The gentle Thetis, and anon behold
The strong-ribb'd bark through liquid mountains
    cut, 40
Bounding between the two moist elements
Like Perseus' horse. Where's then the saucy boat
Whose weak untimber'd sides but even now
Corrival'd greatness? Either to harbor fled
Or made a toast for Neptune. Even so, 45
Doth valor's show and valor's worth divide
In storms of Fortune. For in her ray and brightness
The herd hath more annoyance by the brize
Than by the tiger; but when the splitting wind

24 **artist** scholar. 25 **affin'd** related. 30 **unmingled** pure, not mixed (read here as four syllables). 32 **apply** moralize. 33 **reproof** resistance, refusing to accept. 35 **bauble** weak, toylike. 38 **Boreas** the north wind. 39 **Thetis** originally a sea goddess, here used to mean the sea in general. 42 **Perseus' horse** Pegasus. 46 **valor's . . . worth** apparent bravery and actual bravery. 48 **brize** gadfly.

Makes flexible the knees of knotted oaks,   50
And flies fled under shade, why then the thing of
    courage,
As rous'd with rage, with rage doth sympathize,
And with an accent tun'd in selfsame key
Retorts to chiding Fortune.

  Ulysses.   Agamemnon,   54
Thou great commander, nerve, and bone of Greece,
Heart of our numbers, soul and only spirit
In whom the tempers and the minds of all
Should be shut up, hear what Ulysses speaks.
Besides th' applause and approbation
The which, [*To Agamemnon.*] most mighty for thy
    place and sway,   60
And thou [*To Nestor.*] most reverend for thy
    stretch'd-out life,
I give to both your speeches; which were such
As Agamemnon and the hand of Greece
Should hold up high in brass; and such again
As venerable Nestor, hatch'd in silver,   65
Should with a bond of air, strong as the axletree
In which the heavens ride, knit all Greeks' ears
To his experienc'd tongue; yet let it please both,
Tho great, and wise, to hear Ulysses speak.

  Agamemnon. Speak, Prince of Ithaca, and be't of
    less expect   70
That matter needless, of importless burthen,
Divide thy lips than we are confident,

---

51 **flies fled** flies have fled. **shade** shelter. 54 **Retorts** N. 55 **nerve** sinew. 59 **th' applause** F *the applause:* Q is better metrically since *approbation* has five syllables here. 60 **To Agamemnon** N. 64 **in brass** engraved on a brass tablet. 65 **hatch'd** etched N. 66 **air** breath. 67 **knit** tie, join. 70 **expect** expectation, build-up. 71 **importless** meaningless. **burthen** substance, purport.

When rank Thersites opes his [masty] jaws,
We shall hear music, wit, and oracle.
  Ulysses. Troy, yet upon his basis, had been down,
And the great Hector's sword had lack'd a master
But for these instances.   77
The specialty of rule hath been neglected,
And look how many Grecian tents do stand
Hollow upon this plain, so many hollow factions. 80
When that the general is not like the hive,
To whom the foragers shall all repair,
What honey is expected? Degree being vizarded,
Th' unworthiest shews as fairly in the mask.   84
The heavens themselves, the planets, and this center
Observe degree, priority, and place,
Insisture, course, proportion, season, form,
Office, and custom, in all line of order;
And therefore is the glorious planet Sol
In noble eminence enthron'd and spher'd   90
Amidst the other, whose med'cinable eye
Corrects the ill aspects of planets evil,
And posts, like the commandment of a king,
Sans check, to good and bad. But when the planets
In evil mixture to disorder wander,   95
What plagues and what portents, what mutiny,
What raging of the sea, shaking of earth,
Commotion in the winds! Frights, changes, horrors

73 **rank** vile, offensive. **opes** opens. **masty** massive, powerful; F
Masticke N. 75 **his** its. **basis** base, foundation. **had been** would
have been. 77 **instances** specific causes. 78 **specialty of rule**
prerogatives of ruling or commanding. 83 **Degree** subordination
in rank. **vizarded** masked. 84 **shews** shows. 85 **center** the earth N.
87 **Insisture** regularity, constancy. 89 **Sol** N. 91 **the other** the
other planets. **med'cinable** curative, having the effect of medicine. 92 **aspects** N. 93 **posts** speeds. 94 **Sans check** without
hindrance or hesitation.

Divert and crack, rend and deracinate
The unity and married calm of states   100
Quite from their fixure. O, when degree is shak'd,
Which is the ladder to all high designs,
The enterprise is sick. How could communities,
Degrees in schools, and brotherhoods in cities,
Peaceful commerce from dividable shores,   105
The primogenitive and due of birth,
Prerogative of age, crowns, scepters, laurels,
But by degree, stand in authentic place?
Take but degree away, untune that string,   109
And hark, what discord follows! Each thing meets
In mere oppugnancy. The bounded waters
Should lift their bosoms higher than the shores
And make a sop of all this solid globe.
Strength should be lord of imbecility,
And the rude son should strike his father dead.   115
Force should be right; or rather, right and wrong,
Between whose endless jar justice resides,
Should lose her names, and so should justice too.
Then everything includes itself in power,
Power into will, will into appetite,   120
And appetite, an universal wolf,
So doubly seconded with will and power,
Must make perforce an universal prey
And last eat up himself. Great Agamemnon,
This chaos, when degree is suffocate,   125

99 **deracinate** uproot. 101 **fixure** fixed stability. 102 **designs**
plans, purposes. 105 **dividable** separate. 106 **primogenitive** primo-
geniture. 108 **authentic** true, legal. 111 **oppugnancy** opposition.
112, 114 **Should** would. 113 **sop** a thing soaked or soggy. 114
imbecility physical weakness. 118 **her** their N. 119 **includes itself
in** is embraced in. 125 **suffocate** suffocated.

Follows the choking;
And this neglection of degree is it
That by a pace goes backward in a purpose
It hath to climb. The general's disdain'd
By him one step below, he by the next,   130
That next by him beneath; so every step,
Exampled by the first pace that is sick
Of his superior, grows to an envious fever
Of pale and bloodless emulation.
And 'tis this fever that keeps Troy on foot,   135
Not her own sinews. To end a tale of length,
Troy in our weakness lives, not in her strength.
  Nestor. Most wisely hath Ulysses here discover'd
The fever whereof all our power is sick.
  Agamemnon. The nature of the sickness found,
    Ulysses,   140
What is the remedy?
  Ulysses. The great Achilles, whom opinion crowns,
The sinew and the forehand of our host,
Having his ear full of his airy fame,
Grows dainty of his worth, and in his tent   145
Lies mocking our designs. With him Patroclus
Upon a lazy bed the livelong day
Breaks scurril jests,
And with ridiculous and awkward action
(Which, slanderer, he imitation calls)   150
He pageants us. Sometime, great Agamemnon,
Thy topless deputation he puts on,

128–9 purpose . . . climb N. 132 **sick** envious. 134 **emulation**
envy, imitation (five syllables here). 138 **discover'd** pointed out,
revealed. 142 **opinion** fame, public approval. 143 **forehand** main-
stay. 145 **dainty** fastidious, conceited. 148 **scurril** scurrilous. 151
pageants acts out, mimics. 152 **topless deputation** supreme dignity deputed to the commander.

And like a strutting player whose conceit
Lies in his hamstring and doth think it rich
To hear the wooden dialogue and sound   155
'Twixt his stretch'd footing and the scaffolage—
Such to-be-pitied and orewrested seeming
He acts thy greatness in. And when he speaks,
'Tis like a chime a-mending, with terms unsquar'd,
Which, from the tongue of roaring Typhon dropp'd,
Would [seem] hyperboles. At this fusty stuff 161
The large Achilles, on his press'd bed lolling,
From his deep chest laughs out a loud applause,
Cries 'Excellent! 'Tis Agamemnon just!
Now play me Nestor; hum, and stroke thy beard
As he, being dress'd to some oration.'   166
That's done, as near as the extremest ends
Of parallels, as like as Vulcan and his wife;
Yet god Achilles still cries 'Excellent!
'Tis Nestor right. Now play him me, Patroclus,
Arming to answer in a night alarm.'   171
And then, forsooth, the faint defects of age
Must be the scene of mirth: to cough and spit,
And with a palsy fumbling on his gorget,
Shake in and out the rivet. And at this sport   175
Sir Valor dies; cries 'O, enough, Patroclus!
Or give me ribs of steel; I shall split all

153 **conceit** faculty of mind. 154 **hamstring** tendons behind the
knee, governing leg movement. 156 **stretch'd footing** exaggerated
paces. **scaffolage** wooden stage. 157 **orewrested** too tight,
strained N. 159 **a-mending** being mended. 160 **Typhon** mythical
Greek giant associated with hurricanes. 161 **seem** F *seemes*.
165 **hum** hem and haw. 166 **being dress'd to** preparing for.
oration four syllables. 168 **Vulcan and his wife** N. 170 **me** an
ethical dative, without special meaning. 171 **answer** i.e. answer
a summons to battle. 174 **gorget** a piece of armor for the throat.

In pleasure of my spleen.' And in this fashion
All our abilities, gifts, natures, shapes,
Severals and generals of grace exact,   180
Achievements, plots, orders, preventions,
Excitements to the field, or speech for truce,
Success or loss, what is or is not, serves
As stuff for these two to make paradoxes.
  Nestor. And in the imitation of these twain,   185
Who, as Ulysses says, opinion crowns
With an imperial voice, many are infect.
Ajax is grown self-will'd and bears his head
In such a rein, in full as proud a place
As broad Achilles, and keeps his tent like him,   190
Makes factious feasts, rails on our state of war,
Bold as an oracle, and sets Thersites—
A slave whose gall coins slanders like a mint—
To match us in comparisons with dirt,
To weaken and discredit our exposure,   195
How rank soever rounded in with danger.
  Ulysses. They tax our policy and call it cowardice,
Count wisdom as no member of the war,
Forestall prescience, and esteem no act
But that of hand. The still and mental parts   200
That do contrive how many hands shall strike
When fitness call them on, and know by measure
Of their observant toil the enemies' weight—

178 **spleen** merriment. 180 **Severals . . . exact** particular and
general qualities of excellence. 181 **preventions** defensive meas-
ures. 184 **paradoxes** absurdities. 187 **imperial voice** commanding
influence. **infect** infected. 189 **In such a rein** high, as a horse
tight reined. 190 **broad** arrogant. **keeps** stays in. 195 **exposure**
i.e. to danger. 197 **tax** criticize. 199 **Forestall** obstruct. 202–3
by measure . . . toil by means of their laborious observation
and reconnoitering.

Why, this hath not a finger's dignity.
They call this bedwork, mapp'ry, closet war;   205
So that the ram that batters down the wall,
For the great swing and rudeness of his poise,
They place before his hand that made the engine,
Or those that with the fineness of their souls
By reason guide his execution.   210
  Nestor. Let this be granted, and Achilles' horse
Makes many Thetis' sons.   *Tucket.*
  Agamemnon. What trumpet? Look, Menelaus.
  Menelaus. From Troy.

Enter Aeneas.

  Agamemnon. What would you 'fore our tent?   215
  Aeneas. Is this great Agamemnon's tent, I pray
you?
  Agamemnon. Even this.
  Aeneas. May one that is a herald, and a prince,
Do a fair message to his kingly ears?
  Agamemnon. With surety stronger than Achilles'
arm   220
'Fore all the Greekish heads, which with one voice
Call Agamemnon head and general.
  Aeneas. Fair leave and large security. How may
A stranger to those most imperial looks
Know them from eyes of other mortals?
  Agamemnon.   How?   225
  Aeneas. Ay.
I ask that I might waken reverence,
And on the cheek be ready with a blush
Modest as morning when she coldly eyes
The youthful Phoebus.   230

205 **mapp'ry** map making. 207, 210 **his** its. 208 **his hand that** the
hand of him who. 212 **Thetis' sons** N. **Tucket** a trumpet call.
227 **waken reverence** summon up deferential feelings.

Which is that god in office, guiding men?
Which is the high and mighty Agamemnon?

Agamemnon. This Troyan scorns us, or the men of
    Troy
Are ceremonious courtiers.   234
Aeneas. Courtiers as free, as debonair, unarm'd,
As bending angels; that's their fame in peace.
But when they would seem soldiers, they have galls,
Good arms, strong joints, true swords; and, Jove's
    accord,
Nothing so full of heart. But peace, Aeneas!
Peace, Troyan. Lay thy finger on thy lips.   240
The worthiness of praise distains his worth
If that [the] prais'd himself brings the praise forth.
But what the repining enemy commends,
That breath fame blows; that praise sole pure tran-
    scends.
Agamemnon. Sir, you of Troy, call you yourself
    Aeneas?   245
Aeneas. Ay, Greek, that is my name.
Agamemnon. What's your affair, I pray you?
Aeneas. Sir, pardon; 'tis for Agamemnon's ears.
Agamemnon. He hears nought privately that comes
    from Troy.   249
Aeneas. Nor I from Troy come not to whisper him.
I bring a trumpet to awake his ear,
To set his sense on the attentive bent
And then to speak.
Agamemnon.   Speak frankly as the wind.
It is not Agamemnon's sleeping hour.

236 bending courteous, bowing. 237 galls tempers. 238–9 Jove's
. . . heart N. 241 distains soils, detracts from. 242 the prais'd
F *he prais'd*. 244 sole pure alone and pure. 252 on the attentive
bent at attention.

That thou shalt know, Troyan, he is awake,   255
He tells thee so himself.
  Aeneas.   Trumpet, blow loud.
Send thy brass voice through all these lazy tents,
And every Greek of mettle, let him know
What Troy means fairly shall be spoke aloud.
                      The trumpets sound.
We have, great Agamemnon, here in Troy,   260
A prince call'd Hector—Priam is his father—
Who in this dull and long-continu'd truce
Is rusty grown. He bade me take a trumpet
And to this purpose speak: Kings, princes, lords,
If there be one amongst the fair'st of Greece   265
That holds his honor higher than his ease,
That seeks his praise more than he fears his peril,
That knows his valor and knows not his fear,
That loves his mistress more than in confession,
With truant vows to her own lips he loves,   270
And dare avow her beauty and her worth
In other arms than hers—to him this challenge.
Hector, in view of Troyans and of Greeks,
Shall make it good, or do his best to do it.
He hath a lady wiser, fairer, truer   275
Than ever Greek did compass in his arms,
And will tomorrow with his trumpet call,
Midway between your tents and walls of Troy,
To rouse a Grecian that is true in love.
If any come, Hector shall honor him;   280
If none, he'll say in Troy when he retires,
The Grecian dames are sunburnt and not worth
The splinter of a lance. Even so much.
  Agamemnon. This shall be told our lovers, Lord
    Aeneas.

270 **truant** idle, vain.

29

If none of them have soul in such a kind,   285
We left them all at home. But we are soldiers,
And may that soldier a mere recreant prove,
That means not, hath not, or is not in love.
If then one is, or hath, or means to be,
That one meets Hector; if none else, I'll be he.   290
  Nestor. Tell him of Nestor, one that was a man
When Hector's grandsire suck'd. He is old now,
But if there be not in our Grecian mold
One noble man that hath one spark of fire
To answer for his love, tell him from me,   295
I'll hide my silver beard in a gold beaver
And in my vantbrace put this wither'd brawn,
And meeting him, will tell him that my lady
Was fairer than his grandam, and as chaste
As may be in the world. His youth in flood,   300
I'll [prove] this truth with my three drops of blood.
  Aeneas. Now heavens forbid such scarcity of youth.
  Ulysses. Amen.
  Agamemnon. Fair Lord Aeneas, let me touch your
    hand;
To our pavilion shall I lead you first.   305
Achilles shall have word of this intent,
So shall each lord of Greece from tent to tent.
Yourself shall feast with us before you go
And find the welcome of a noble foe.
       Exeunt. [*Manent*] *Ulysses and Nestor.*
  Ulysses. Nestor.   310
  Nestor. What says Ulysses?
  Ulysses. I have a young conception in my brain;

296 **beaver** helmet with face guard. 297 **vantbrace** armor for the
arms. 300 **His youth in flood** though he be in his prime. 301
prove F pawn. SD **Manent** F *Manet:* Q omits. 312 **young conception** germ of an idea.
    30

Be you my time to bring it to some shape.
  Nestor. What is't?
  Ulysses. This 'tis: 315
Blunt wedges rive hard knots. The seeded pride
That hath to this maturity blown up
In rank Achilles must or now be cropp'd
Or, shedding, breed a nursery of like evil
To overbulk us all.
  Nestor.   Well, and how?   320
  Ulysses. This challenge that the gallant Hector
    sends,
However it is spread in general name,
Relates in purpose only to Achilles.
  Nestor. The purpose is perspicuous even as sub-
    stance,
Whose grossness little characters sum up;   325
And, in the publication, make no strain
But that Achilles, were his brain as barren
As banks of Lybia (though Apollo knows
'Tis dry enough), will with great speed of judgment,
Ay, with celerity, find Hector's purpose   330
Pointing on him.
  Ulysses.   And wake him to the answer, think you?
  Nestor. Yes, 'tis most meet. Who may you else op-
    pose
That can from Hector bring his honor off,
If not Achilles? Though't be a sportful combat,

316 **rive** split, sever. **seeded** mature, gone to seed. 318 **or** either.
319 **nursery** read 'nurs'ry.' 324 **perspicuous** clear, evident. **even**
read 'e'en.' **substance** material riches. 325 **characters** figures.
326 **publication** the proclamation of Hector's challenge. **make no
strain** never fear, have no difficulty in believing. 328 **Lybia** North
African desert country. 332 **meet** fitting. 333 **bring . . . off** come
out with honor unscathed.

Yet in this trial much opinion dwells;   335
For here the Troyans taste our dear'st repute
With their fin'st palate; and trust to me, Ulysses,
Our imputation shall be oddly pois'd
In this wild action. For the success,
Although particular, shall give a scantling   340
Of good or bad unto the general,
And in such indexes, although small pricks
To their subsequent volumes, there is seen
The baby figure of the giant mass
Of things to come at large. It is suppos'd   345
He that meets Hector issues from our choice;
And choice, being mutual act of all our souls,
Makes merit her election and doth boil,
As 'twere, from forth us all, a man distill'd
Out of our virtues; who miscarrying,   350
What heart from hence receives the conqu'ring part
To steel a strong opinion to themselves!
Which entertain'd, limbs are in his instruments,
In no less working, than are swords and bows   354
Directive by the limbs.

   Ulysses.   Give pardon to my speech:
Therefore 'tis meet Achilles meet not Hector.
Let us, like merchants, show our foulest wares
And think perchance they'll sell; if not,
The lustre of the better yet to show

---

335 **opinion** reputation. 338 **imputation** good name. **oddly pois'd** in delicate balance. 339–41 **For . . . general** N. 339 **success** outcome. 340 **scantling** portion, amount. 342–5 **And in . . . large** N. 343 **subsequent** stressed — $\stackrel{\prime}{-}$ —. 348 **Makes . . . election** elects the one with greatest merit. 351 **conqu'ring part** the winning side, i.e. the Trojan. 352 **steel** bolster up. 353–5 **Which . . . the limbs** N. 355 **Directive** subject to direction, directable. 359 **to show** to be shown.

Shall show the better. Do not consent   360
That ever Hector and Achilles meet;
For both our honor and our shame in this
Are dogg'd with two strange followers.
  Nestor. I see them not with my old eyes. What are
    they?
  Ulysses. What glory our Achilles shares from Hec-
    tor,   365
Were he not proud, we all should wear with him.
But he already is too insolent,
And we were better parch in Afric sun
Than in the pride and salt scorn of his eyes
Should he 'scape Hector fair. If he were foil'd,   370
Why then we did our main opinion crush
In taint of our best man. No, make a lott'ry,
And by device let blockish Ajax draw
The sort to fight with Hector. Among ourselves
Give him allowance as the worthier man,   375
For that will physic the great Myrmidon
Who broils in loud applause, and make him fall
His crest that prouder than blue iris bends.
If the dull brainless Ajax come safe off,
We'll dress him up in voices; if he fail,   380
Yet go we under our opinion still,
That we have better men. But hit or miss,
Our project's life this shape of sense assumes,
Ajax employ'd plucks down Achilles' plumes.   384
  Nestor. Now, Ulysses, I begin to relish thy advice,

---

369 **salt** bitter. 371 **main opinion** chief reason for our glorious
reputation. 372 **taint** the staining of honor. 373 **device** stratagem.
blockish stupid. 374 **sort** lot. 375 **allowance** acknowledgment.
376 **physic** cure. **great Myrmidon** Achilles. 377 **broils in** seethes
in, revels in. **fall** lower, let fall. 380 **voices** loud praises.

And I will give a taste of it forthwith
To Agamemnon. Go we to him straight.
Two curs shall tame each other. Pride alone
Must tarre the mastiffs on, as 'twere their bone. 389
Exeunt.

389 **tarre** urge, incite.

34

Act II

SCENE 1

Enter Ajax and Thersites.

Ajax. Thersites?

Thersites. Agamemnon—how if he had biles, full, all over, generally?

Ajax. Thersites? 4

Thersites. And those biles did run? Say so. Did not the general run? Were not that a botchy core?

Ajax. Dog!

Thersites. Then there would come some matter from him. I see none now. 9

    Ajax. Thou bitch-wolf's son, canst [thou] not hear? Feel, then!   *Strikes him.*

Thersites. The plague of Greece upon thee, thou mongrel, beef-witted lord!

Ajax. Speak then, you whinid'st leaven, speak! I will beat thee into handsomeness. 15

Thersites. I shall sooner rail thee into wit and holiness; but I think thy horse will sooner con an oration than you learn a prayer without book. Thou canst strike, canst thou? A red murrain [o'] thy jade's tricks. 20

---

2 **biles** boils. 6 **botchy** ulcerous. 8 **matter** pun on 'sense' and 'pus.' 10 **canst thou** F *canst* y^u. 14 **whinid'st** finewed'st, most mouldy N. 15 **handsomeness** politeness. 17 **con** learn. 18 **without book** by heart. 19 **murrain** plague. **o'** F *o'th.* 20 **jade's tricks** tricks of a mean horse.

35

Ajax. Toadstool, learn me the proclamation.

Thersites. Dost thou think I have no sense, thou strik'st me thus?

Ajax. The proclamation!

Thersites. Thou art proclaim'd a fool, I think.   25

Ajax. Do not, porpentine, do not! My fingers itch.

Thersites. I would thou didst itch from head to foot, and I had the scratching of thee. I would make thee the loathsom'st scab in Greece.

Ajax. I say, the proclamation!   30

Thersites. Thou grumblest and railest every hour on Achilles, and thou art as full of envy at his greatness as Cerberus is at Proserpina's beauty; ay, that thou bark'st at him.

Ajax. Mistress Thersites!   35

Thersites. Thou shouldst strike him.

Ajax. Cobloaf!

Thersites. He would pun thee into shivers with his fist, as a sailor breaks a bisquit.

Ajax. You whoreson cur!   40

Thersites. Do, do!

Ajax. Thou stool for a witch!

Thersites. Ay, do, do, thou sodden-witted lord! Thou hast no more brain than I have in mine elbows. An asinico may tutor thee. Thou scurvy valiant ass, thou art here but to thrash Troyans, and thou art bought and sold among those of any wit like a barbarian slave. If thou use to beat me, I will begin at

---

21 **learn me** inform me of. 22 **sense** sensibility, feeling. 26 **porpentine** porcupine. 33 **Cerberus . . . Proserpina's** N. 37 **Cobloaf** small, rounded loaf. 38 **pun** pound. 45 **asinico** young ass. 47 **bought and sold** manipulated and deceived as of no account.

thy heel and tell what thou art by inches, thou thing
of no bowels, thou! 50

Ajax. You dog!

Thersites. You scurvy lord!

Ajax. You cur!

Thersites. Mars his idiot! Do, rudeness; do, camel,
do do! 55

Enter Achilles and Patroclus.

Achilles. Why, how now, Ajax? Wherefore do you
this? How now, Thersites? What's the matter, man?

Thersites. You see him there, do you?

Achilles. Ay. What's the matter?

Thersites. Nay, look upon him. 60

Achilles. So I do. What's the matter?

Thersites. Nay, but regard him well.

Achilles. Well? Why, I do so.

Thersites. But yet you look not well upon him; for
whomsoever you take him to be, he is Ajax. 65

Achilles. I know that, fool.

Thersites. Ay, but that fool knows not himself.

Ajax. Therefore I beat thee. 68

Thersites. Lo, lo, lo, lo, what modicums of wit he
utters. His evasions have ears thus long. I have
bobb'd his brain more than he has beat my bones. I
will buy nine sparrows for a penny, and his piamater
is not worth the ninth part of a sparrow. This lord,
Achilles, Ajax—who wears his wit in his belly, and
his guts in his head—I'll tell you what I say of him.

Achilles. What? 76

Thersites. I say this Ajax—

---

54 **Mars his idiot** Mars' idiot N. 70 **evasions . . . long** they are
asslike, stupid. 71 **bobb'd** beaten, pummeled. 72 **piamater** brain.

Achilles. Nay, good Ajax.

Thersites. Has not so much wit—

Achilles. Nay, I must hold you.   80

Thersites. As will stop the eye of Helen's needle, for whom he comes to fight.

Achilles. Peace, fool.

Thersites. I would have peace and quietness, but the fool will not—he, there! That he! Look you there!   86

Ajax. O thou damn'd cur, I shall—

Achilles. Will you set your wit to a fool's?

Thersites. No, I warrant you, for a fool's will shame it.   90

Patroclus. Good words, Thersites.

Achilles. What's the quarrel?

Ajax. I bade [the] vile owl go learn me the tenor of the proclamation, and he rails upon me

Thersites. I serve thee not.   95

Ajax. Well, go to, go to.

Thersites. I serve here voluntary.

Achilles. Your last service was sufferance, 'twas not voluntary; no man is beaten voluntary. Ajax was here the voluntary, and you as under an impress.

Thersites. Ene so, a great deal of your wit, too, lies in your sinews, or else there be liars. Hector shall have a great catch if he knock out either of your brains. He were as good crack a fusty nut with no kernel.   105

Achilles. What, with me too, Thersites?

Thersites. There's Ulysses and old Nestor, whose wit was moldy ere their grandsires had nails on their

88 set oppose. 93 the vile F *thee vile.* 100 impress forced service. 101 Ene even. 102 be are. 104 He were as good he might as well. fusty stale.

38

toes, yoke you like draft oxen and make you plough
up the war.   110

Achilles. What? What?

Thersites. Yes, good sooth. To Achilles! to Ajax!
to—

Ajax. I shall cut out your tongue.   114

Thersites. 'Tis no matter; I shall speak as much as
thou afterwards.

Patroclus. No more words, Thersites.

Thersites. I will hold my peace when Achilles'
brooch bids me, shall I?

Achilles. There's for you, Patroclus.   120

Thersites. I will see you hang'd like clotpolls ere I
come any more to your tents. I will keep where there
is wit stirring and leave the faction of fools.   *Exit.*

Patroclus. A good riddance.

Achilles. Marry, this, sir, is proclaim'd through all
    our host: 125
That Hector, by the fifth hour of the sun,
Will with a trumpet 'twixt our tents and Troy
Tomorrow morning call some knight to arms
That hath a stomach, and such a one that dare
Maintain—I know not what. 'Tis trash. Farewell.

Ajax. Farewell? Who shall answer him?   131

Achilles. I know not. 'Tis put to lottery; otherwise
he knew his man.

Ajax. O, meaning you? I will go learn more of it.
                              [Exeunt.]

---

112 **good sooth** in truth, surely. **To Achilles! to Ajax!** N. 119
brooch N. 121 **clotpolls** blockheads. 129 **stomach** appetite for
fighting. 133 **knew** would know. SD **Exeunt** F *Exit;* Q omits.

SCENE 2

Enter Priam, Hector, Troilus, Paris, and Helenus.

Priam. After so many hours, lives, speeches spent,
Thus once again says Nestor from the Greeks:
'Deliver Helen, and all damage else
(As honor, loss of time, travail, expense,
Wounds, friends, and what else dear that is con-
    sum'd   **5**
In hot digestion of this cormorant war)
Shall be stroke off.' Hector, what say you to't?
Hector. Though no man lesser fears the Greeks
    than I,
As far as touches my particular,
Yet dread Priam,   **10**
There is no lady of more softer bowels,
More spongy to suck in the sense of fear,
More ready to cry out, 'Who knows what follows?'
Than Hector is. The wound of peace is surety,
Surety secure. But modest doubt is call'd   **15**
The beacon of the wise, the tent that searches
To th' bottom of the worst. Let Helen go.
Since the first sword was drawn about this question,
Every tithe soul 'mongst many thousand dismes
Hath been as dear as Helen. I mean, of ours.   **20**
If we have lost so many tenths of ours
To guard a thing not ours, nor worth to us,

---

6 **cormorant** a predatory bird. 9 **touches my particular** concerns
me in particular. 11 **softer bowels** sensitivity, compassion. 14
surety overconfident security. 16 **tent** swab for probing wounds.
19 **tithe** tenth N. **dismes** (pronounced 'dimes') tens (of men lost).
40

Had it our name, the value of one ten,
What merit's in that reason which denies
The yielding of her up.
  Troilus.   Fie, fie, my brother!   25
Weigh you the worth and honor of a king
So great as our dread father in a scale
Of common ounces? Will you with counters sum
The past proportion of his infinite,
And buckle in a waist most fathomless   30
With spans and inches so diminutive
As fears and reason? Fie, for godly shame!
  Helenus. No marvel, though you bite so sharp at
    reasons,
You are so empty of them. Should not our father
Bear the great sway of his affairs with reasons,   35
Because your speech hath none that tells him so.
  Troilus. You are for dreams and slumbers, brother
    priest;
You fur your gloves with reason. Here are your rea-
    sons:
You know an enemy intends you harm;
You know a sword employ'd is perilous   40
And reason flies the object of all harm.
Who marvels, then, when Helenus beholds
A Grecian and his sword, if he do set
The very wings of reason to his heels,
And fly like chidden Mercury from Jove   45
Or like a star disorb'd? Nay, if we talk of reason,

23 Had it our name even if she were one of us. **28 counters** beads
on an abacus. **29 past** exceeding. **infinite** infinite greatness. **30
fathomless** measureless. **33 reasons** homophonous pun on
'reasons' and 'raisins.' **38 fur . . . reason** use reason for everything. **45 And fly . . . Jove** N. **46 disorb'd** displaced from its
orbit.

Let's shut our gates and sleep. Manhood and honor
Should have hard hearts, would they but fat their
    thoughts
With this cramm'd reason. Reason and respect
Make livers pale and lustihood deject.   50
  Hector. Brother, she is not worth what she doth
    cost
The holding.
  Troilus.   What's aught, but as 'tis valu'd?
  Hector. But value dwells not in particular will.
It holds his estimate and dignity
As well wherein 'tis precious of itself   55
As in the prizer. 'Tis [mad] idolatry
To make the service greater than the god,
And the will dotes that is inclinable
To what infectiously itself affects,
Without some image of th' affected merit.   60
  Troilus. I take today a wife, and my election
Is led on in the conduct of my will;
My will enkindled by mine eyes and ears,
Two traded pilots 'twixt the dangerous shores
Of will and judgment. How may I avoid,   65
Although my will distaste what it elected,
The wife I chose? There can be no evasion
To blench from this, and to stand firm by honor.
We turn not back the silks upon the merchant

---

48 **fat** make fat, feed. 49 **respect** circumspection. 50 **livers** the
reputed source of courage and 'gall.' **deject** dejected. 53 **particular
will** the volition of an individual. 54 **his** its. **dignity** worthiness.
56 **prizer** person who prizes. **mad** F *made.* 58–60 And the . . .
merit N. 58 **dotes** is foolish. 64 **traded** experienced. 65 **avoid**
cast off. 66 **distaste** not like. 68 **blench** flinch.

When we have spoil'd them; nor the remainder
    viands   70
We do not throw in unrespective [sieve]
Because we now are full. It was thought meet
Paris should do some vengeance on the Greeks.
Your breath of full consent bellied his sails.
The seas and winds, old wranglers, took a truce   75
And did him service. He touch'd the ports desir'd,
And for an old aunt whom the Greeks held captive,
He brought a Grecian queen whose youth and fresh-
    ness
Wrinkles Apollo's and makes stale the morning.
Why keep we her? The Grecians keep our aunt.   80
Is she worth keeping? Why, she is a pearl
Whose price hath launch'd above a thousand ships,
And turn'd crown'd kings to merchants.
If you'll avouch 'twas wisdom Paris went,
As you must needs, for you all cried, 'Go, go';   85
If you'll confess he brought home noble prize,
As you must needs, for you all clapp'd your hands
And cried, 'Inestimable'; why do you now
The issue of your proper wisdoms rate
And do a deed that fortune never did,   90
Beggar the estimation which you priz'd
Richer than sea and land? O theft most base
That we have stolne what we do fear to keep!
But thieves unworthy of a thing so stolne,
That in their country did them that disgrace,   95
We fear to warrant in our native place.

71 **sieve** F *same*. 76 **touch'd** reached. 77 **old aunt** cf. I.2.13 N.
79 **Wrinkles** makes appear wrinkled and ugly. 89 **issue** result.
rate berate, chide. 91 **Beggar** make poor, belittle. 93 **That** in that.
stolne stol'n. 96 **warrant** make good, defend.

Enter Cassandra with her hair about her ears.

Cassandra. Cry, Troyans, cry!
Priam.   What noise? What shriek is this?
Troilus. 'Tis our mad sister. I do know her voice.
Cassandra. Cry, Troyans!
Hector. It is Cassandra.   100
Cassandra. Cry, Troyans, cry! Lend me ten thou-
     sand eyes
And I will fill them with prophetic tears.
Hector. Peace, sister, peace.
Cassandra. Virgins and boys, mid-age and wrinkled
     old,
Soft infancy, that nothing can but cry,   105
Add to my clamor! Let us pay betimes
A moity of that mass of moan to come.
Cry, Troyans, cry! Practice your eyes with tears.
Troy must not be, nor goodly Ilion stand.
Our firebrand brother Paris burns us all.   110
Cry, Troyans, cry; a Helen and a woe.
Cry, cry, Troy burns, or else let Helen go.   *Exit.*
  Hector. Now, youthful Troilus, do not these high
     strains
Of divination in our sister work
Some touches of remorse? Or is your blood   115
So madly hot that no discourse of reason
Nor fear of bad success in a bad cause
Can qualify the same?
  Troilus.   Why, brother Hector,
We may not think the justness of each act
Such and no other than event doth form it,   120

107 **moity** moiety, part. 116 **discourse of reason** process of
reasoning. 117 **success** result, final issue.
   44

Nor once deject the courage of our minds
Because Cassandra's mad. Her brainsick raptures
Cannot distaste the goodness of a quarrel
Which hath our several honors all engag'd
To make it gracious. For my private part,   125
I am no more touch'd than all Priam's sons,
And Jove forbid there should be done amongst us
Such things as might offend the weakest spleen
To fight for and maintain.

   Paris. Else might the world convince of levity   130
As well my undertakings as your counsels;
But I attest the gods, your full consent
Gave wings to my propension and cut off
All fears attending on so dire a project.
For what, alas, can these my single arms?   135
What propugnation is in one man's valor
To stand the push and enmity of those
This quarrel would excite? Yet I protest,
Were I alone to pass the difficulties,
And had as ample power as I have will,   140
Paris should nere retract what he hath done
Nor faint in the pursuit.

   Priam.   Paris, you speak
Like one besotted on your sweet delights.
You have the honey still, but these the gall;
So to be valiant is no praise at all.   145

   Paris. Sir, I propose not merely to myself
The pleasure such a beauty brings with it;

122 **raptures** ecstatic visions. 123 **distaste** destroy the savor of.
125 **gracious** righteous. 128 **spleen** heart, courage. 130 **convince**
convict. 132 **attest** call to witness. 133 **propension** inclination,
desire. 135 **can** can do. **single** unaided. 136 **propugnation** defense.
139 **pass** experience, bear the brunt of. 141 **nere** never. **retract**
draw back from.

But I would have the soil of her fair rape
Wip'd off in honorable keeping her.
What treason were it to the ransack'd queen,   150
Disgrace to your great worths, and shame to me,
Now to deliver her possession up
On terms of base compulsion! Can it be
That so degenerate a strain as this   154
Should once set footing in your generous bosoms?
There's not the meanest spirit on our party
Without a heart to dare, or sword to draw,
When Helen is defended; nor none so noble
Whose life were ill bestow'd or death unfam'd
Where Helen is the subject. Then, I say,   160
Well may we fight for her whom we know well
The world's large spaces cannot parallel.

   Hector. Paris and Troilus, you have both said well;
And on the cause and question now in hand
Have gloz'd, but superficially; not much   165
Unlike young men, whom Aristotle thought
Unfit to hear moral philosophy.
The reasons you allege do more conduce
To the hot passion of distemp'red blood
Than to make up a free determination   170
'Twixt right and wrong; for pleasure and revenge
Have ears more deaf than adders to the voice
Of any true decision. Nature craves
All dues be rend'red to their owners. Now
What nearer debt in all humanity   175
Than wife is to the husband? If this law
Of nature be corrupted through affection,

148 **soil** stain. **rape** abduction. 150 **ransack'd** abducted. 155
generous high-born. 156 **on our party** on our side. 165 **gloz'd**
commented. 166 **Aristotle** N. 172 **adders** N. 177 **affection** appetite,
inclination.

And that great minds, of partial indulgence
To their benumbed wills, resist the same,
There is a law in each well ord'red nation   180
To curb those raging appetites that are
Most disobedient and refractory.
If Helen then be wife to Sparta's king,
As it is known she is, these moral laws
Of nature and of nation speak aloud   185
To have her back return'd. Thus to persist
In doing wrong extenuates not wrong,
But makes it much more heavy. Hector's opinion
Is this in way of truth. Yet neretheless,
My spritely brethren, I propend to you   190
In resolution to keep Helen still;
For 'tis a cause that hath no mean dependence
Upon our joint and several dignities.
   Troilus. Why, there you touch'd the life of our design.
Were it not glory that we more affected   195
Than the performance of our heaving spleens,
I would not wish a drop of Troyan blood
Spent more in her defense. But worthy Hector,
She is a theme of honor and renown,
A spur to valiant and magnanimous deeds,   200
Whose present courage may beat down our foes,
And fame in time to come canonize us.
For I presume brave Hector would not lose
So rich advantage of a promis'd glory
As smiles upon the forehead of this action   205
For the wide world's revenue.

178 **partial** excessive (three syllables here). 189 **neretheless** nevertheless. 190 **propend** bow to, give in to. 196 **heaving spleens** unruly feelings of resentment. 202 **canonize** stressed — ´ —. 206 **revenue** stressed — ´ —.

Hector.   I am yours,
You valiant offspring of great Priamus.
I have a roisting challenge sent amongst
The dull and factious nobles of the Greeks
Will strike amazement to their drowsy spirits.   210
I was advertis'd their great general slept,
Whilst emulation in the army crept.
This I presume will wake him.   *Exeunt*.

SCENE 3

Enter Thersites solus.

Thersites. How now, Thersites? What, lost in the
labyrinth of thy fury? Shall the elephant Ajax
carry it thus? He beats me, and I rail at him. O
worthy satisfaction! Would it were otherwise; that
I could beat him whilst he rail'd at me. 'Sfoot, I'll
learn to conjure and raise divels, but I'll see some
issue of my spiteful execrations. Then there's Achilles, a rare enginer! If Troy be not taken till these
two undermine it, the walls will stand till they fall
of themselves. O thou great thunder-darter of Olym-
pus, forget that thou art Jove, the king of gods;
and Mercury, loose all the serpentine craft of thy
caduceus, if thou take not that little little less than
little wit from them that they have, which short-
arm'd ignorance itself knows is so abundant scarce

208 **roisting** roistering, bullying. 210 **Will** which will. **amazement** wonder, bewilderment. 211 **advertis'd** informed (stressed
— ´ —). 212 **emulation** ambitious rivalry. 3 **carry it** behave
himself. 5 **'Sfoot** 'God's foot,' a mild oath. 6 **but** unless. 8 **enginer**
a contriver of military engines. 13 **caduceus** Mercury's wand.
14–5 **short-arm'd** incapable of reaching far.

48

it will not in circumvention deliver a fly from a
spider without drawing the massy irons and cutting
the web. After this, the vengeance on the whole
camp! Or rather the bone ache, for that, methinks,
is the curse dependent on those that war for a
placket. I have said my prayers and divel, Envy, say
'Amen.' What ho? My Lord Achilles?   22

Enter Patroclus.

Patroclus. Who's there? Thersites? Good Thersites,
come in and rail.   24
Thersites. If I could have rememb'red a gilt counterfeit, thou wouldst not have slipp'd out of my
contemplation. But it is no matter. Thyself upon
thyself! The common curse of mankind, folly and
ignorance, be thine in great revenue! Heaven bless
thee from a tutor, and discipline come not near
thee. Let thy blood be thy direction till thy death,
then if she that lays thee out says thou art a fair
corse, I'll be sworn and sworn upon't she never
shrouded any but lazars. Amen. Where's Achilles?
Patroclus. What, art thou devout? Wast thou in
a prayer?   36
Thersites. Ay. The heavens hear me!

Enter Achilles.

Achilles. Who's there?
Patroclus. Thersites, my lord.   39
Achilles. Where, where? Art thou come? Why, my
cheese, my digestion, why hast thou not serv'd thy-

17 **massy irons** great swords. 19 **bone ache** syphilis. 21 **placket**
petticoat, woman. 25–6 **gilt counterfeit . . . slipp'd** N. 29 **bless**
preserve. 31 **blood** passion. 33 **corse** corpse. 34 **lazars** lepers.
41 **cheese** N.

self into my table so many meals? Come, what's
Agamemnon?

Thersites. Thy commander, Achilles. Then tell me,
Patroclus, what's Achilles?   45

Patroclus. Thy lord, Thersites. Then tell me, I pray
thee, what's thyself?

Thersites. Thy knower, Patroclus. Then tell me,
Patroclus, what art thou?

Patroclus. Thou mayst tell that know'st.   50

Achilles. O, tell, tell!

Thersites. I'll decline the whole question. Agamemnon commands Achilles, Achilles is my lord, I am
Patroclus' knower, and Patroclus is a fool.

Patroclus. You rascal!   55

Thersites. Peace, fool, I have not done.

Achilles. He is a privileg'd man. Proceed, Thersites.

Thersites. Agamemnon is a fool, Achilles is a fool,
Thersites is a fool, and, as aforesaid, Patroclus is a
fool.   61

Achilles. Derive this. Come.

Thersites. Agamemnon is a fool to offer to command Achilles; Achilles is a fool to be commanded
of Agamemnon; Thersites is a fool to serve such a
fool; and Patroclus is a fool positive.   66

Patroclus. Why am I a fool?

*Enter Agamemnon, Ulysses, Nestor, Diomedes,
Ajax, and Calchas.*

Thersites. Make that demand to the Creator; it
suffices me thou art. Look you, who comes here?

---

52 **decline** run through (as in grammatical declining). 62 **Derive**
explain, show reasons. 65 **of** by. 68 **demand** question.

Achilles. Patroclus, I'll speak with nobody. Come in with me, Thersites. *Exit.*

Thersites. Here is such patchery, such juggling, and such knavery! All the argument is a cuckold and a whore—a good quarrel to draw emulations, factions, and bleed to death upon. Now the dry suppeago on the subject, and war and lechery confound all! [*Exit.*]

Agamemnon. Where is Achilles? 78

Patroclus. Within his tent but ill dispos'd, my lord.

Agamemnon. Let it be known to him that we are here.

He [shent] our messengers and we lay by
Our appertainments, visiting of him.
Let him be told [so, lest] perchance he think
We dare not move the question of our place 84
Or know not what we are.

Patroclus. I shall so say to him.
[*Exit.*]

Ulysses. We saw him at the opening of his tent. He is not sick. 87

Ajax. Yes, lion-sick, sick of proud heart. You may call it mlancholy if [you] will favor the man; but, by my head, it is pride. But why? Why? Let him show us the cause A word, my lord 91

Nestor. What moves Ajax thus to bay at him?

Ulysses. Achilles hath inveigled his fool from him.

Nestor. Who, Thersites?

Ulysses. He. 95

72 patchery roguery. 76 suppeago serpigo (a skin disease). SD Exit not in F or Q. 81 shent reviled, scolded; F *sent;* Q *sate.* N. 82 appertainments rights, prerogatives. 83 so, lest F *of, so.* 84 move assert. place position of authority. 85 Exit not in F or Q. 89 you F omits.

Nestor. Then will Ajax lack matter, if he have lost his argument.

Ulysses. No. You see he is his argument that has his argument, Achilles.   99

Nestor. All the better; their fraction is more our wish than their faction. But it was a strong counsel that a fool could disunite.

Ulysses. The amity that wisdom knits not, folly may easily untie.

Enter Patroclus.

Here comes Patroclus.   105

Nestor. No Achilles with him?

Ulysses. The elephant hath joints, but none for courtesy. His legs are legs for necessity, not for [flexure].   109

Patroclus. Achilles bids me say he is much sorry
If anything more than your sport and pleasure
Did move your greatness and this noble state
To call upon him. He hopes it is no other
But for your health and your digestion sake,   114
And after-dinner's breath.

Agamemnon.   Hear you, Patroclus.
We are too well acquainted with these answers.
But his evasion, wing'd thus swift with scorn,
Cannot outfly our apprehensions.
Much attribute he hath, and much the reason
Why we ascribe it to him; yet all his virtues,   120

96–9 matter . . . **Achilles** N. 100 **fraction** division, separation.
101 **faction** uniting together as friends. **counsel** N. 103 **knits not,**
N. 109 **flexure** bending; F *flight* N. 114 **digestion** digestion's.
115 **breath** exercise. 118 **apprehensions** here five syllables. 119
attribute reputation, praise.

Not virtuously of his own part beheld,
Do in our eyes begin to lose their gloss;
[Yea, like] fair fruit in an unwholesome dish,
Are like to rot untasted. Go and tell him
We came to speak with him; and you shall not sin
If you do say we think him overproud   126
And underhonest, in self-assumption greater
Than in the note of judgment. And worthier than
        himself
Here tends the savage strangeness he puts on,
Disguise the holy strength of their command,   130
And underwrite in an observing kind
His humorous predominance, yea, watch
His pettish lines, his ebbs, his flows, as if
The passage and whole carriage of this action
Rode on his tide. Go tell him this, and add   135
That if he overhold his price so much,
We'll none of him. But let him, like an engine
Not portable, lie under this report:
Bring action hither; this cannot go to war.
A stirring dwarf we do allowance give   140
Before a sleeping giant. Tell him so.
    Patroclus. I shall, and bring his answer presently.
                                            [*Exit.*]
    Agamemnon. In second voice we'll not be satisfied;

121 **Not . . . beheld** not looked at or considered on his part in
the proper way. 123 **Yea, like** F *Yea, and like.* 128 **note of
judgment** mark of good judgment. 128–32 **And worthier . . .
predominance** N. 129 **tends** awaits. **savage strangeness** rude
aloofness. 131 **underwrite** submit to. 132 **humorous** capricious.
133 **lines** lunes, fits of temper. 136 **overhold** overestimate. 140
allowance praise, approbation. 142 **presently** at once. SD **Exit**
not in F or Q. 143 **second voice** his words repeated by another
person, words at second hand.

We come to speak with him. Ulysses, enter you.

Exit Ulysses.

Ajax. What is he more than another? 145

Agamemnon. No more than what he thinks he is.

Ajax. Is he so much? Do you not think he thinks himself a better man than I am?

Agamemnon. No question.

Ajax. Will you subscribe his thought and say he is? 151

Agamemnon. No, noble Ajax. You are as strong, as valiant, as wise, no less noble, much more gentle, and altogether more tractable.

Ajax. Why should a man be proud? How doth pride grow? I know not what it is. 156

Agamemnon. Your mind is the clearer, Ajax, and your virtues the fairer. He that is proud eats up himself. Pride is his own glass, his own trumpet, his own chronicle; and whatever praises itself but in the deed, devours the deed in the praise. 161

Enter Ulysses.

Ajax. I do hate a proud man as I hate the engend'ring of toads.

Nestor. Yet he loves himself. Is't not strange?

Ulysses. Achilles will not to the field tomorrow.

Agamemnon. What's his excuse?

Ulysses.   He doth rely on none,
But carries on the stream of his dispose 167
Without observance or respect of any,
In will peculiar and in self-admission.

---

159 **his** its. **glass** mirror. 160 **chronicle** history. 167 **dispose** predisposition. 169 **peculiar** unique, a law unto himself. **self-admission** self-approbation.

Agamemnon. Why, will he not upon our fair re-
    quest   170
Untent his person and share the air with us?
Ulysses. Things small as nothing, for request's sake
    only,
He makes important. Possess'd he is with greatness,
And speaks not to himself, but with a pride
That quarrels at self-breath. Imagin'd [worth]   175
Holds in his blood such swolne and hot discourse
That 'twixt his mental and his active parts
Kingdom'd Achilles in commotion rages
And batters gainst itself. What should I say?   179
He is so plaguy proud that the death tokens of it
Cry, 'No recovery.'
  Agamemnon.   Let Ajax go to him.
Dear lord, go you and greet him in his tent.
'Tis said he holds you well and will be led
At your request a little from himself.
  Ulysses. O Agamemnon, let it not be so!   185
We'll consecrate the steps that Ajax makes
When they go from Achilles. Shall the proud lord
That bastes his arrogance with his own seam
And never suffers matter of the world
Enter his thoughts—save such as do revolve   190
And ruminate himself—shall he be worshipp'd
Of what we hold an idol more than he?
No, this thrice worthy and right valiant lord
Must not so stale his palm, nobly acquir'd,
Nor by my will assubjugate his merit,   195

172 **for request's sake** merely because they are requested. 175
self-breath his own words. **worth** F *wroth*. 176 **swolne** swollen.
discourse quarrel, controversy. 178 **Kingdom'd** N. 188 **seam**
grease, drippings. 192 **Of what we hold** by him whom we regard.
194 **stale** cheapen. **palm** honors. 195 **assubjugate** debase.

As amply titled as Achilles is,
By going to Achilles.
That were to enlard his fat-already pride
And add more coals to Cancer, when he burns
With entertaining great Hyperion.   200
This lord go to him? Jupiter forbid,
And say in thunder, 'Achilles go to him!'

  Nestor. [*Aside.*] O, this is well! He rubs the vein of
    him.

  Diomedes. [*Aside.*] And how his silence drinks up
    this applause!

  Ajax. If I go to him, with my armed fist I'll pash
him ore the face   206

  Agamemnon.   O no, you shall not go.

  Ajax. And a be proud with me, I'll feeze his pride.
Let me go to him.

  Ulysses. Not for the worth that hangs upon our
    quarrel.   210

  Ajax. A paltry insolent fellow.

  Nestor. [*Aside.*] How he describes himself!

  Ajax. Can he not be sociable?

  Ulysses. [*Aside.*] The raven chides blackness.

  Ajax. I'll let his humor's blood.   215

  Agamemnon. [*Aside.*] He will be the physician
that should be the patient.

  Ajax. And all men were o' my mind—

  Ulysses. [*Aside.*] Wit would be out of fashion.

  Ajax. A should not bear it so; a should eat swords
first. Shall pride carry it?   221

---

198 **to enlard** to fatten; read 't'enlard.' 199 **coals to Cancer** N.
205 **pash** bash, strike. 208 **a** he; so also in l. 220. **feeze** settle,
chastise. 215 **let his humor's blood** relieve him of humorous blood
by bleeding N. 220 **eat swords** N.

Nestor. [*Aside.*] And 'twould, you'ld carry half.

Ulysses. [*Aside.*] A would have ten shares.

Ajax. I will knead him. I'll make him supple.   224

Nestor. [*Aside.*] He's not yet through warm. Force him with praises. Pour in, pour in; his ambition is dry.

Ulysses. [*To Agamemnon.*] My lord, you feed too
    much on this dislike.

Nestor. Our noble general, do not do so.   229

Diomedes. You must prepare to fight without
    Achilles.

Ulysses. Why, 'tis this naming of him doth him
    harm.

Here is a man—but 'tis before his face;

I will be silent.

Nestor.   Wherefore should you so?   233

He is not emulous, as Achilles is.

Ulysses. Know the whole world, he is as valiant.

Ajax. A whoreson dog, that shall palter thus with us. Would he were a Troyan!

Nestor. What a vice were it in Ajax now—   238

Ulysses. If he were proud.

Diomedes. Or covetous of praise.

Ulysses. Ay, or surly borne.

Diomedes. Or strange, or self-affected.

Ulysses. Thank the heavens, lord, thou art of sweet
    composure.   243

Praise him that got thee, she that gave thee suck;

---

223 **shares** i.e. as of stock N. 225 **He's . . . warm** N. **through** thoroughly. **Force** farce, stuff. 228 **My lord** N. 234 **emulous** envious. 236 **palter** shuffle, dodge. 241 **surly borne** of surly bearing. 242 **strange** aloof. **self-affected** egotistical. 244 **got** begot.

[Fam'd] be thy tutor, and thy parts of nature
Thrice fam'd beyond, beyond all erudition.
But he that disciplin'd thy arms to fight,
Let Mars divide eternity in twain   248
And give him half; and for thy vigor,
Bull-bearing Milo his addition yield
To sinewy Ajax. I will not praise thy wisdom,
Which, like a bourn, a pale, a shore, confines
Thy spacious and dilated parts. Here's Nestor   253
Instructed by the antiquary times;
He must, he is, he cannot but be wise.
But pardon, father Nestor, were your days
As green as Ajax' and your brain so temper'd,
You should not have the eminence of him   258
But be as Ajax.
   Ajax.   Shall I call you father?
   Ulysses. Ay, my good son.
   Diomedes.   Be rul'd by him, Lord Ajax.
   Ulysses. There is no tarrying here; the hart Achilles
Keeps thicket. Please it our general,
To call together all his state of war.   263
Fresh kings are come to Troy; tomorrow
We must with all our main of power stand fast.
And here's a lord—come knights from East to West
And cull their flower, Ajax shall cope the best.   267
   Agamemnon. Go we to counsel. Let Achilles sleep.
Light boats may sail swift, though greater bulks
            draw deep.   *Exeunt.*

245 **Fam'd** F *Fame.* 250 **Milo** N. **addition** particular quality
(i.e. of strength). 252 **bourn** boundary. **pale** fence. 253 **dilated
parts** expansive qualities of excellence. 254 **antiquary** ancient.
257 **green** young, few. 258 **should . . . eminence of** would not
be superior to. 265 **main** strength. 267 **cope** meet.

Act III

SCENE 1

Music sounds within.

Enter Pandarus and a Servant.

Pandarus. Friend, you! Pray you, a word. Do not you follow the young Lord Paris?

Servant. Ay, sir, when he goes before me.

Pandarus. You depend upon him, I mean.

Servant. Sir, I do depend upon the Lord.   5

Pandarus. You depend upon a noble gentleman; I must needs praise him.

Servant. The Lord be praised.

Pandarus. You know me, do you not?

Servant. Faith, sir, superficially.   10

Pandarus. Friend, know me better; I am the Lord Pandarus.

Servant. I hope I shall know your honor better.

Pandarus. I do desire it.

Servant. You are in the state of grace?   15

Pandarus. Grace? Not so, friend. Honor and lordship are my title. What music is this?

Servant. I do but partly know, sir; it is music in parts.

Pandarus. Know you the musicians?   20

Servant. Wholly, sir.

Pandarus. Who play they to?

---

2 **follow** i.e. as a servant, follower. 13 **honor** N. 19 **in parts in** harmony.

59

Servant. To the hearers, sir.

Pandarus. At whose pleasure, friend?   24

Servant. At mine, sir, and theirs that love music.

Pandarus. Command, I mean, friend.

Servant. Who shall I command, sir?

Pandarus. Friend, we understand not one another. I am too courtly and thou art too cunning. At whose request do these men play?   30

Servant. That's to't indeed, sir. Marry, sir, at the request of Paris my lord, who's there in person; with him the mortal Venus, the heartblood of beauty, love's invisible soul.

Pandarus. Who? My cousin Cressida?   35

Servant. No, sir; Helen. Could you not find out that by her attributes?

Pandarus. It should seem, fellow, that thou hast not seen the Lady Cressida. I come to speak with Paris from the Prince Troilus. I will make a complimental assault upon him, for my business seethes.

Servant. Sodden business! There's a stewed phrase indeed!   43

Enter Paris and Helena.

Pandarus. Fair be to you, my lord, and to all this fair company. Fair desires in all fair measure fairly guide them, especially to you, fair queen! Fair thoughts be your fair pillow.   47

Helen. Dear lord, you are full of fair words.

Pandarus. You speak your fair pleasure, sweet queen. Fair prince, here is good broken music.   50

Paris. You have broke it, cousin, and by my life

34 love's invisible soul N. 40–1 complimental assault N. 42 Sodden N. SD Helena N. 44 Fair N. 50 broken music music in parts, harmony.

you shall make it whole again. You shall piece it out with a piece of your performance. Nell, he is full of harmony.

Pandarus. Truly, lady, no.   55

Helen. O, sir—

Pandarus. Rude, in sooth; in good sooth, very rude.

Paris. Well said, my lord, well. You say so in fits.

Pandarus. I have business to my lord, dear queen. My lord, will you vouchsafe me a word?   60

Helen. Nay, this shall not hedge us out. We'll hear you sing, certainly.

Pandarus. Well, sweet queen, you are pleasant with me. But, marry, thus, my lord: my dear lord and most esteemed friend, your brother Troilus—   65

Helen. My Lord Pandarus, honey sweet lord—

Pandarus. Go to, sweet queen, go to. —Commends himself most affectionately to you—

Helen. You shall not bob us out of our melody; if you do, our melancholy upon your head.   70

Pandarus. Sweet queen, sweet queen! That's a sweet queen, i' faith—

Helen. And to make a sweet lady sad is a sour offense.   74

Pandarus. Nay, that shall not serve your turn; that shall it not, in truth, la! Nay, I care not for such words; no, no. —And, my lord, he desires you that if the king call for him at supper, you will make his excuse.

Helen. My Lord Pandarus!   80

Pandarus. What says my sweet queen, my very, very sweet queen?

---

57 **sooth** truth. 58 **fits** N. 61 **hedge us out** put us off. 69 **bob** cheat

Paris. What exploit's in hand? Where sups he to-night?

Helen. Nay, but my lord— 85

Pandarus. What says my sweet queen? My cousin will fall out with you.

Helen. You must not know where he sups.

Paris. With my disposer, Cressida. 89

Pandarus. No, no; no such matter. You are wide. Come, your disposer is sick.

Paris. Well, I'll make excuse.

Pandarus. Ay, good my lord. Why should you say Cressida? No, your poor disposer's sick.

Paris. I spy! 95

Pandarus. You spy? What do you spy? Come, give me an instrument now, sweet queen.

Helen. Why, this is kindly done.

Pandarus. My niece is horrible in love with a thing you have, sweet queen. 100

Helen. She shall have it, my lord, if it be not my Lord Paris.

Pandarus. He? No, she'll none of him; they two are twain. 104

Helen. Falling in after falling out may make them three.

Pandarus. Come, come, I'll hear no more of this. I'll sing you a song now.

Helen. Ay, ay, prithee now. By my troth, sweet lord, thou hast a fine forehead. 110

Pandarus. Ay, you may, you may.

Helen. Let the song be love; this love will undo us all. O, Cupid, Cupid, Cupid!

88 Helen N. 89 **disposer** mistress, lady. 90 **wide** wide of the truth, have missed the mark. 104 **twain** separated by disagreements, at variance.

Pandarus. Love? Ay, that it shall, i' faith.

Paris. Ay, good now; love, love, nothing but love.

Pandarus. In good troth, it begins so. 116

> Love, love, nothing but love, still more!
>> For O, love's bow
>> Shoots buck and doe.
>> The shaft confounds 120
>> Not that it wounds
>> But tickles still the sore.
>> These lovers cry;
>> O ho, they die!
> Yet that which seems the wound to kill, 125
>> Doth turn 'O ho!' to 'Ha, ha, he!'
>> So dying love lives still.
>> O ho! awhile, but ha, ha, ha!
> O ho! groans out for ha, ha, ha!—Hey ho! 129

Helen. In love, i' faith, to the very tip of the nose!

Paris. He eats nothing but doves, love, and that breeds hot blood, and hot blood begets hot thoughts, and hot thoughts beget hot deeds, and hot deeds is love. 134

Pandarus. Is this the generation of love? Hot blood, hot thoughts, and hot deeds? Why, they are vipers! Is love a generation of vipers? Sweet lord, who's afield today? 138

Paris. Hector, Deiphobus, Helenus, Antenor, and all the gallantry of Troy. I would fain have arm'd today but my Nell would not have it so. How chance my brother Troilus went not? 142

Helen. He hangs the lip at something. You know all, Lord Pandarus?

---

115 **Love** N. 120 **confounds** destroys. 121 **that** that which. 125 **wound to kill** killing wound. 131 **doves** N. 137 **vipers** N.

Pandarus. Not I, honey sweet queen. I long to hear how they sped today. You'll remember your brother's excuse?   147

Paris. To a hair.

Pandarus. Farewell, sweet queen.

Helen. Commend me to your niece.   150

Pandarus. I will, sweet queen.   [*Exit.*]

Sound a retreat.

Paris. They're come from field. Let us to Priam's
    hall
To greet the warriors. Sweet Helen, I must woo you
To help unarm our Hector. His stubborn buckles,
With these your white enchanting fingers touch'd,
Shall more obey than to the edge of steel   156
Or force of Greekish sinews. You shall do more
Than all the island kings—disarm great Hector.

Helen. 'Twill make us proud to be his servant, Paris.
Yea, what he shall receive of us in duty   160
Gives us more palm in beauty than we have,
Yea, overshines ourself.

Paris. Sweet, above thought I love thee!   *Exeunt.*

SCENE 2

Enter Pandarus and Troilus' Man.

Pandarus. How now? Where's thy master? At my cousin Cressida's?

Man. No, sir; he stays for you to conduct him thither.

---

151 **Exit** not in F or Q. 158 **island** i.e. the Greek islands. 161 **palm** renown. 163 **Sweet . . . thee** N. 3 **stays** waits.

Enter Troilus.

Pandarus. O, here he comes. How now, how now?
Troilus. Sirrah, walk off.   6
Pandarus. Have you seen my cousin?
Troilus. No, Pandarus. I stalk about her door
Like a strange soul upon the Stygian banks
Staying for waftage. O, be thou my Charon   10
And give me swift transportance to those fields
Where I may wallow in the lily beds
Propos'd for the deserver. O gentle Pandarus,
From Cupid's shoulder pluck his painted wings
And fly with me to Cressid.   15
Pandarus. Walk here i' th' orchard. I'll bring her
         straight.   *Exit Pandarus.*
Troilus. I am giddy; expectation whirls me round.
Th' imaginary relish is so sweet
That it enchants my sense. What will it be
When that the wat'ry palates taste indeed   20
Love's thrice repured nectar? Death, I fear me,
Sounding destruction, or some joy too fine,
Too subtle, potent, and too sharp in sweetness
For the capacity of my ruder powers.
I fear it much, and I do fear besides   25
That I shall lose distinction in my joys,
As doth a battle when they charge on heaps
The enemy flying.   28

Enter Pandarus.

6 **Sirrah** a term of address used to inferiors. 9–10 **Stygian . . .
Charon** N. 10 **waftage** passage. 13 **Propos'd** promised. 16 **straight**
immediately. 21 **repured** refined; F *reputed.* 22 **Sounding** swooning. 27 **battle** army. 27 **on heaps** in great numbers.

Pandarus. She's making her ready; she'll come straight. You must be witty now. She does so blush, and fetches her wind so short, as if she were fray'd with a sprite. I'll fetch her. It is the prettiest villain; she fetches her breath so short as a new-tane sparrow.   *Exit Pandarus.*

Troilus. Even such a passion doth embrace my
        bosom.   35
My heart beats thicker than a feverous pulse,
And all my powers do their bestowing lose,
Like vassalage at unawares encount'ring
The eye of majesty.   39

Enter Pandarus and Cressida.

Pandarus. Come, come, what need you blush? Shame's a baby. Here she is now; swear the oaths now to her that you have sworn to me. What, are you gone again? You must be watch'd ere you be made tame, must you? Come your ways, come your ways. And you draw backward, we'll put you i' th' fills. Why do you not speak to her? Come, draw this curtain and let's see your picture. Alas, the day! How loath you are to offend daylight! And 'twere dark you'ld close sooner. So, so, rub on, and kiss the mistress. How now? A kiss in fee-farm? Build there, carpenter; the air is sweet. Nay, you shall fight your hearts out ere I part you. The falcon as the tercel, for all the ducks i' th' river. Go to, go to!

31 **fetches her wind** breathes. **fray'd** frightened. 32 **It** she (baby talk). 33 **new-tane** newly taken or captured. 35 **Even** read 'e'en.' 36 **thicker** faster. 37 **bestowing** use, employment. 43 **watch'd** kept from sleeping N. 46 **fills** shafts, as of a horse-drawn wagon. 47 **curtain** veil. 49 **close** come together. **rub on** press on (a term from bowling). 50 **in fee-farm** indefinitely N. 52–3 **falcon . . . tercel** N.

Troilus. You have bereft me of all words, lady.

Pandarus. Words pay no debts. Give her deeds. But she'll bereave you o' th' deeds too, if she call your activity in question. What, billing again? Here's 'In witness whereof the parties interchangeably—' Come in, come in! I'll go get a fire. [*Exit.*]

Cressida. Will you walk in, my lord?   60

Troilus. O Cressida, how often have I wish'd me thus!

Cressida. Wish'd, my lord? The gods grant—O my lord!

Troilus. What should they grant? What makes this pretty abruption? What too curious dreg espies my sweet lady in the fountain of our love?   67

Cressida. More dregs than water, if my tears have eyes.

Troilus. Fears make divels of cherubins; they never see truly.   71

Cressida. Blind fear that seeing reason leads finds [safer] footing than blind reason stumbling without fear. To fear the worst oft cures the worse.

Troilus. O, let my lady apprehend no fear. In all Cupid's pageant there is presented no monster.   76

Cressida. [Nor] nothing monstrous neither?

Troilus. Nothing but our undertakings, when we vow to weep seas, live in fire, eat rocks, tame tigers; thinking it harder for our mistress to devise imposition enough than for us to undergo any difficulty imposed. This is the monstruosity in love, lady; that

---

58–9 'In . . . interchangeably' a legal phrase used in mutual contracts. SD **Exit** not in F or Q. 66 **abruption** breaking off. 66 **curious** minute. 73 **safer** F *safe*. 76 **pageant** masque, pantomime. 77 **Nor** F *Not*. 82 **monstruosity** monstrosity.

the will is infinite and the execution confin'd; that the desire is boundless and the act a slave to limit.

Cressida. They say all lovers swear more performance than they are able, and yet reserve an ability that they never perform, vowing more than the perfection of ten, and discharging less than the tenth part of one. They that have the voice of lions and the act of hares, are they not monsters?   90

Troilus. Are there such? Such are not we! Praise us as we are tasted; allow us as we prove. Our head shall go bare till merit crown it. No perfection in reversion shall have a praise in present. We will not name desert before his birth, and being born, his addition shall be humble. Few words to fair faith. Troilus shall be such to Cressid. As what envy can say worst shall be a mock for his truth; and what truth can speak truest, not truer than Troilus.

Cressida. Will you walk in, my lord?   100

Enter Pandarus.

Pandarus. What, blushing still? Have you not done talking yet?

Cressida. Well, uncle, what folly I commit I dedicate to you.   104

Pandarus. I thank you for that. If my lord get a boy of you, you'll give him me. Be true to my lord. If he flinch, chide me for it.

Troilus. You know now your hostages—your uncle's word and my firm faith.   109

Pandarus. Nay, I'll give my word for her too. Our kindred though they be long ere they are woo'd,

83 will desire, appetite. 92 tasted tested. allow estimate. 93–4 in reversion in the future. 96 his its. 97–8 envy . . . his truth N. 105 get beget.

they are constant being won. They are burrs, I can
tell you; they'll stick where they are thrown.

   Cressida. Boldness comes to me now and brings me
     heart.

Prince Troilus, I have lov'd you night and day   115
For many weary months.

   Troilus. Why was my Cressid then so hard to win?

   Cressida. Hard to seem won. But I was won, my
     lord,

With the first glance that ever—pardon me!
If I confess much you will play the tyrant.   120
I love you now, but not till now so much
But I might master it. In faith, I lie.
My thoughts were like unbridled children [grown]
Too headstrong for their mother. See, we fools!
Why have I blabb'd? Who shall be true to us   125
When we are so unsecret to ourselves?
But though I lov'd you well, I woo'd you not;
And yet, good faith, I wish'd myself a man,
Or that we women had men's privilege   129
Of speaking first. Sweet, bid me hold my tongue,
For in this rapture I shall surely speak
The thing I shall repent. See, see, your silence,
Coming in dumbness, from my weakness draws
My soul of counsel from me. Stop my mouth.   134

   Troilus. And shall, albeit sweet music issues thence.

   Pandarus. Pretty, i' faith.

   Cressida. My lord, I do beseech you, pardon me;
'Twas not my purpose thus to beg a kiss.
I am asham'd. O heavens, what have I done!
For this time will I take my leave, my lord.   140

   Troilus. Your leave, sweet Cressid?

123 grown F *grow.* 133 **Coming** forward, apt N. 134 **soul of
counsel** innermost thoughts.

Pandarus. Leave! And you take leave till tomorrow morning—

Cressida. Pray you, content you.

Troilus. What offends you, lady? 145

Cressida. Sir, mine own company.

Troilus. You cannot shun yourself.

Cressida.   Let me go and try.
I have a kind of self resides with you;
But an unkind self, that itself will leave
To be another's fool. Where is my wit? 150
I would be gone. I speak I know not what.

Troilus. Well know they what they speak that
    [speak] so wisely.

Cressida. Perchance, my lord, I shew more craft
    than love,
And fell so roundly to a large confession
To angle for your thoughts. But you are wise, 155
Or else you love not; for to be wise and love
Exceeds man's might. That dwells with gods above.

Troilus. Oh, that I thought it could be in a woman
(As if it can, I will presume in you)
To feed for aye her lamp and flames of love; 160
To keep her constancy in plight and youth,
Outliving beauties outward, with a mind
That doth renew swifter than blood decays;
Or that persuasion could but thus convince me
That my integrity and truth to you 165
Might be affronted with the match and weight
Of such a winnowed [purity] in love.
How were I then uplifted! But, alas,

152 **speak so** F *speaks so.* 154 **roundly** frankly, straight-forwardly.
161 **in plight and youth** in health and youth, ever young. 162
beauties outward external beauties. 166 **affronted** met with,
matched with. 167 **purity** F *puriritie.*

I am as true as truth's simplicity,
And simpler than the infancy of truth.   170
  Cressida. In that I'll war with you.
  Troilus.   O virtuous fight,
When right with right wars who shall be most right.
True swains in love shall in the world to come
Approve their truths by Troilus. When their rhymes,
Full of protest, of oath, and big compare,   175
Wants similies, truth tir'd with iteration—
As true as steel, as plantage to the moon,
As sun to day, as turtle to her mate,
As iron to adamant, as earth to th' center—
Yet after all comparisons of truth,   180
As truth's authentic author to be cited,
'As true as Troilus' shall crown up the verse,
And sanctify the numbers.
  Cressida.   Prophet may you be!
If I be false, or swerve a hair from truth,
When time is old and hath forgot itself,   185
When water drops have worn the stones of Troy
And blind oblivion swallow'd cities up,
And mighty states characterless are grated
To dusty nothing; yet let memory
From false to false among false maids in love   190
Upbraid my falsehood. When they've said 'As false
As air, as water, as wind, as sandy earth,
As fox to lamb, as wolf to heifer's calf,
Pard to the hind, or stepdame to her son,'

---

174 **Approve** attest, confirm. 175 **protest** stressed — ´. **compare** comparisons. 176 **Wants** want; cf. I.3.8 N. 177 **plantage** plants, vegetation N. 178 **turtle** turtle dove. 179 **adamant** loadstone. 188 **characterless** stressed — ´ — —. 194 **Pard** leopard.

Yea, let them say, to stick the heart of falsehood,
'As false as Cressid.'   196

Pandarus. Go to, a bargain made! Seal it, seal it.
I'll be the witness. Here I hold your hand, here my
cousin's. If ever you prove false one to another,
since I have taken such pains to bring you together,
let all pitiful goers-between be call'd to the world's
end after my name. Call them all Pandars. Let all
constant men be Troiluses, all false women Cressids,
and all brokers-between Pandars! Say 'Amen.'

Troilus. Amen.   205

Cressida. Amen.

Pandarus. Amen. Whereupon I will shew you a
chamber, which bed, because it shall not speak of
your pretty encounters, press it to death. Away!
And Cupid grant all tongue-tied maidens here   210
Bed, chamber, and Pandar to provide this gear.

                                                    Exeunt.

SCENE 3

*Enter Ulysses, Diomedes, Nestor, Agamemnon,
Menelaus, and Calchas. Flourish.*

Calchas. Now, princes, for the service I have done
            you,
Th' advantage of the time prompts me aloud
To call for recompense. Appear it to your mind
That through the sight I bear in things to love,
I have abandon'd Troy, left my possession,   5
Incurr'd a traitor's name, expos'd myself
From certain and possess'd conveniences

195 stick stab. SD Exeunt N. SD Flourish fanfare. 4 sight . . .
love N. 5 possession property.

To doubtful fortunes, sequest'ring from me all
That time, acquaintance, custom, and condition
Made tame and most familiar to my nature; 10
And here, to do you service, am become
As new into the world, strange, unacquainted.
I do beseech you, as in way of taste,
To give me now a little benefit
Out of those many regist'red in promise 15
Which, you say, live to come in my behalf.

   Agamemnon. What wouldst thou of us, Troyan?
    Make demand.

   Calchas. You have a Troyan prisoner call'd An-
    tenor,
Yesterday took. Troy holds him very dear.
Oft have you (often have you thanks therefore) 20
Desir'd my Cressid in right great exchange,
Whom Troy hath still denied. But this Antenor
I know is such a wrest in their affairs
That their negotiations all must slack,
Wanting his manage; and they will almost 25
Give us a prince of blood, a son of Priam,
In change of him. Let him be sent, great princes,
And he shall buy my daughter, and her presence
Shall quite strike off all service I have done
In most accepted pain.

   Agamemnon.   Let Diomedes bear him 30
And bring us Cressid hither. Calchas shall have
What he requests of us. Good Diomed,
Furnish you fairly for this interchange.

8 **sequest'ring** setting aside. 10 **tame** usual, familiar. 13 **taste**
sample. 16 **live to come** exist to be used in the future. 23 **wrest**
vital instrument; cf. I.3.157 N. 25 **Wanting his manage** lacking
his management. 30 **pain** hardships N. **bear** take. 33 **Furnish you**
equip yourself.

Withal bring word if Hector will tomorrow
Be answer'd in his challenge. Ajax is ready.   35
  Diomedes. This shall I undertake, and 'tis a bur-
    then
Which I am proud to bear.   *Exit.*

    Enter Achilles and Patroclus in their tent.

  Ulysses. Achilles stand i' th' entrance of his tent.
Please it our general to pass strangely by him
As if he were forgot; and princes all,   40
Lay negligent and loose regard upon him.
I will come last. 'Tis like he'll question me
Why such unplausive eyes are bent, why turn'd on
    him.
If so, I have derision medicinable
To use between your strangeness and his pride, 45
Which his own will shall have desire to drink.
It may do good. Pride hath no other glass
To show itself but pride; for supple knees
Feed arrogance and are the proud man's fees.
  Agamemnon. We'll execute your purpose and put
    on   50
A form of strangeness as we pass along.
So do each lord, and either greet him not
Or else disdainfully, which shall shake him more
Than if not look'd on. I will lead the way.
  Achilles. What, comes the general to speak with
    me?   55
You know my mind. I'll fight no more 'gainst Troy.
  Agamemnon. What says Achilles? Would he ought
    with us?

39 **strangely** aloofly. 41 **loose** disrespectful, negligent. 42 **like**
likely. 43 **unplausive** not applauding, disapproving. 44 **medicinable** pronounced 'med'cinable.' 47 **glass** mirror.

Nestor. Would you, my lord, ought with the general?

Achilles. No.

Nestor. Nothing, my lord.   60

Agamemnon. The better.

              [*Exeunt Agamemnon and Nestor.*]

Achilles. Good day, good day.

Menelaus. How do you? How do you?   [*Exit.*]

Achilles. What, does the cuckold scorn me?

Ajax. How now, Patroclus?   65

Achilles. Good morrow, Ajax.

Ajax. Ha.

Achilles. Good morrow.

Ajax. Ay, and good next day too.   [*Exit.*]

Achilles. What mean these fellows? Know they not
    Achilles?   70

Patroclus. They pass by strangely. They were us'd
    to bend
To send their smiles before them to Achilles,
To come as humbly as they us'd to creep
To holy altars.

  Achilles.   What, am I poor of late?   74
'Tis certain, greatness, once falne out with fortune,
Must fall out with men too. What the declin'd is
He shall as soon read in the eyes of others
As feel in his own fall; for men, like butterflies,
Shew not their mealy wings but to the summer;
And not a man for being simply man   80
Hath any honor, but honor'd for those honors
That are without him, as place, riches, and favor,
Prizes of accident as oft as merit;

69 **Exit** F *Exeunt;* this blanket SD is the F substitute for the
several exits supplied by modern editors at ll. 61 and 63. 75 **falne**
fall'n. 82 **without him** outside of him.

Which when they fall, as being slippery standers,
The love that lean'd on them as slippery too,   85
Doth one pluck down another, and together
Die in the fall. But 'tis not so with me;
Fortune and I are friends. I do enjoy
At ample point all that I did possess,   89
Save these men's looks, who do, methinks, find out
Something not worth in me such rich beholding
As they have often given. Here is Ulysses.
I'll interrupt his reading. How now, Ulysses?
  Ulysses. Now, great Thetis' son.
  Achilles.   What are you reading?
  Ulysses. A strange fellow here   95
Writes me that man, how dearly ever parted,
How much in having, or without or in,
Cannot make boast to have that which he hath,
Nor feels not what he owes, but by reflection;
As when his virtues shining upon others   100
Heat them, and they retort that heat again
To the first giver.
  Achilles.   This is not strange, Ulysses.
The beauty that is borne here in the face
The bearer knows not, but commends itself
[To others' eyes; nor doth the eye itself,   105
That most pure spirit of sense, behold itself,]
Not going from itself; but eye to eye oppos'd
Salutes each other with each other's form.
For speculation turns not to itself
Till it hath travel'd and is married there   110
Where it may see itself. This is not strange at all.

89 **At ample point** fully. 96 **how . . . parted** howsoever well
supplied with parts, or talents. 97 **or . . . or** either . . . or.
99 **owes** owns. 101 **retort** return. 105–6 **To . . . itself** not in F.
109 **speculation** seeing, sight. 110 **married** joined.

Ulysses. I do not strain at the position—
It is familiar—but at the author's drift;
Who in his circumstance expressly proves
That no [man] is the lord of anything.   115
Though in and of him there is much consisting,
Till he communicate his parts to others,
Nor doth he of himself know them for aught
Till he behold them formed in th' applause
Where [th' are] extended; who, like an arch, rever-
    b'rate   120
The voice again, or like a gate of steel,
Fronting the sun, receives and renders back
His figure and his heat. I was much rapt in this,
And apprehended here immediately
The unknown Ajax.   125
Heavens, what a man is there! A very horse,
That has he knows not what. Nature, what things
    there are
Most abject in regard and dear in use!
What things again most dear in the esteem
And poor in worth! Now shall we see tomorrow   130
An act that very chance doth throw upon him—
Ajax renown'd. O heavens, what some men do,
While some men leave to do!
How some men creep in skittish Fortune's hall
Whiles others play the idiots in her eyes!   135
How one man eats into another's pride,
While pride is feasting in his wantonness!

112 **strain** F *straine it.* 113 **drift** general direction of the author's
argument. 114 **circumstance** detailed proof. 115 **man** F *may.*
116 **consisting** residing, inhering. 120 **th' are** F *they are.* 120
extended magnified, spread. 120 **arch** vaulted roof. 127 **Nature**
a mild oath or expletive. 128 **abject** poor, mean. 128 **dear in use**
precious in the using. 134–5 **How . . . eyes** N. 137 **feasting** N.

To see these Grecian lords! Why, even already
They clap the lubber Ajax on the shoulder
As if his foot were on brave Hector's breast   140
And great Troy shrinking.
   Achilles.   I do believe it,
For they pass'd by me as misers do by beggars,
Neither gave to me good word nor look.
What, are my deeds forgot?   144
   Ulysses. Time hath, my lord, a wallet at his back
Wherein he puts alms for Oblivion,
A great-siz'd monster of ingratitudes.
Those scraps are good deeds past,
Which are devour'd as fast as they are made,
Forgot as soon as done. Perseverance, dear my lord,
Keeps honor bright. To have done is to hang   151
Quite out of fashion like a rusty mail,
In monumental mock'ry. Take the instant way,
For honor travels in a strait so narrow
Where one but goes abreast. Keep then the path;
For emulation hath a thousand sons   156
That one by one pursue. If you give way
Or hedge aside from the direct forthright,
Like to an ent'red tide, they all rush by
And leave you hindmost;   160
Or like a gallant horse falne in the first rank
Lie there for pavement to the abject [rear],
Orerun and trampled on. Then what they do in present,
Though less than yours in past, must oretop yours.

139 **lubber** lout, blockhead. 145 **wallet** large bag. 146 **alms** gifts
(i.e. the *scraps* of l. 148). **Oblivion** secondary accent on last
syllable. 152 **mail** coat of mail. 153 **instant** present. 155 **one but**
only one. **goes** walks. 156 **emulation** rivalry. 158 **forthright**
straightaway. 162 **rear** rear ranks N.

For Time is like a fashionable host   165
That slightly shakes his parting guest by th' hand,
And with his arms outstretch'd, as he would fly,
Grasps in the comer. The welcome ever smiles,
And [farewell] goes out sighing. O, let not virtue
    seek
Remuneration for the thing it was;   170
For beauty, wit,
High birth, vigor of bone, desert in service,
Love, friendship, charity, are subjects all
To envious and calumniating time.   174
One touch of nature makes the whole world kin:
That all with one consent praise new-born gauds
Though they are made and molded of things past,
And [give] to dust that is a little gilt
More laud than gilt oredusted.
The present eye praises the present object.   180
Then marvel not, thou great and complete man,
That all the Greeks begin to worship Ajax,
Since things in motion [sooner] catch the eye
Than what not stirs. The cry went out on thee,
And still it might, and yet it may again,   185
If thou wouldst not entomb thyself alive
And case thy reputation in thy tent,
Whose glorious deeds, but in these fields of late,
Made emulous missions 'mongst the gods themselves
And drave great Mars to faction.
    Achilles.   Of this my privacy
I have strong reasons.
    Ulysses.   But 'gainst your privacy
The reasons are more potent and heroical.   192

169 **farewell** F *farewels*. 175 **touch** quality, trait. 178 **give** N.
181 **complete** whole, perfect (stressed ´ —). 183 **sooner** F *begin
to* N. 184 **out on** Q *once on*. 189 **emulous** envious. 190 **drave** drove.

79

'Tis known, Achilles, that you are in love
With one of Priam's daughters.
   Achilles. Ha? Known?   195
   Ulysses. Is that a wonder?
The providence that's in a watchful state
Knows almost every grain of Pluto's gold,
Finds bottom in th' uncomprehensive deeps,
Keeps place with thought, and almost like the gods
[Does] thoughts unveil in their dumb cradles.   201
There is a mystery, with whom relation
Durst never meddle, in the soul of state,
Which hath an operation more divine
Than breath or pen can give expressure to.   205
All the commerce that you have had with Troy
As perfectly is ours as yours, my lord.
And better would it fit Achilles much
To throw down Hector than Polixena.   209
But it must grieve young Pyrrhus now at home,
When fame shall in [our islands] sound her trump
And all the Greekish girls shall tripping sing,
'Great Hector's sister did Achilles win,
But our great Ajax bravely beat down him.'
Farewell, my lord. I as your lover speak;   215
The fool slides ore the ice that you should break.
                                 [*Exit.*]
   Patroclus. To this effect, Achilles, have I mov'd
    you.

---

198 **Knows . . . gold** N. 199 **uncomprehensive** incomprehensible.
200 **Keeps place with** consorts with. 201 **Does** Q *Do;* F *Doe.*
202 **relation** act of relating, telling. 203 **state** the State. 205 **expressure** expression. 206 **commerce** stressed — ´—. 209 **Polixena**
N. 210 **Pyrrhus** Neoptolemus, son of Achilles. 211 **our islands**
F *her island.* 211 **trump** trumpet. 216 **fool . . . break** N.

A woman impudent and mannish grown
Is not more loath'd than an effeminate man
In time of action. I stand condemn'd for this;   220
They think my little stomach to the war
And your great love to me restrains you thus.
Sweet, rouse yourself; and the weak wanton Cupid
Shall from your neck unloose his amorous fold,
And like a dew drop from the lion's mane   225
Be shook to airy air.
   Achilles.   Shall Ajax fight with Hector?
   Patroclus. Ay, and perhaps receive much honor by
    him.
   Achilles. I see my reputation is at stake;
My fame is shrowdly gor'd.
   Patroclus.   O then, beware.   229
Those wounds heal ill that men do give themselves.
Omission to do what is necessary
Seals a commission to a blank of danger,
And danger like an ague subtly taints
Even then when we sit idly in the sun.   234
   Achilles. Go call Thersites hither, sweet Patroclus.
I'll send the fool to Ajax and desire him
T' invite the Troyan lords after the combat
To see us here unarm'd. I have a woman's longing,
An appetite that I am sick withal,
To see great Hector in his weeds of peace,   240

Enter Thersites.

To talk with him and to behold his visage,
Even to my full of view. A labor sav'd.
   Thersites. A wonder.

221 **stomach** liking. 224 **fold** embrace. 229 **shrowdly gor'd** sharply
(shrewdly) wounded. 232 **commission . . . blank** N. 234, 242
Even read 'e'en.' 240 **weeds** clothes.

81

Achilles. What?   244

Thersites. Ajax goes up and down the field asking for himself.

Achilles. How so?

Thersites. He must fight singly tomorrow with Hector, and is so prophetically proud of an heroical cudgeling that he raves in saying nothing.   250

Achilles. How can that be?

Thersites. Why, he stalks up and down like a peacock—a stride and a stand; ruminates like an hostess that hath no arithmetic but her brain to set down her reckoning; bites his lip with a politic regard, as who should say, 'There were wit in this head and 'twould out'; and so there is, but it lies as coldly in him as fire in a flint, which will not show without knocking. The man's undone forever; for if Hector break not his neck i' th' combat, he'll break't himself in vainglory. He knows not me. I said, 'Good morrow, Ajax'; and he replies, 'Thanks, Agamemnon.' What think you of this man that takes me for the general? He's grown a very land-fish, languageless, a monster. A plague of opinion! A man may wear it on both sides, like a leather jerkin.   266

Achilles. Thou must be my ambassador to him, Thersites.

Thersites. Who, I? Why, he'll answer nobody. He professes not answering. Speaking is for beggars; he wears his tongue in's arms. I will put on his pres-

255 **reckoning** bill, computation. 255–6 **political regard** serious look. 256 **were** is. 257 **and** if. **'twould** it would come; F *twoo'd.* 264 **land-fish** a fish living on land, an unnatural creature. 265 **of** on. 265 **opinion** reputation, fame. 271 **put on** act out.

ence; let Patroclus make his demands to me; you
shall see the pageant of Ajax.   273

Achilles. To him, Patroclus. Tell him I humbly desire the valiant Ajax to invite the most valorous
Hector to come unarm'd to my tent, and to procure
safe-conduct for his person of the magnanimous and
most illustrious, six-or-seven-times-honor'd captain,
general of the Grecian army, Agamemnon, et cetera.
Do this.   280

Patroclus. Jove bless great Ajax!

Thersites. Hum.

Patroclus. I come from the worthy Achilles.

Thersites. Ha?

Patroclus. Who most humbly desires you to invite
Hector to his tent.   286

Thersites. Hum.

Patroclus. And to procure safe-conduct from Agamemnon.

Thersites. Agamemnon?   290

Patroclus. Ay, my lord.

Thersites. Ha!

Patroclus. What say you to't?

Thersites. God buy you, with all my heart.

Patroclus. Your answer, sir.   295

Thersites. If tomorrow be a fair day, by eleven
o'clock it will go one way or other. Howsoever, he
shall pay for me ere he has me.

Patroclus. Your answer, sir.

Thersites. Fare you well, with all my heart.   300

Achilles. Why, but he is not in this tune, is he?

Thersites. No, but he's out o' tune thus. What
music will be in him when Hector has knock'd out his

294 buy be with; cf. *Shakespeare's Pronunciation*, p. 329.

brains, I know not, but I am sure, none, unless the
fiddler Apollo get his sinews to make catlings on.

Achilles. Come, thou shalt bear a letter to him
straight.   307

Thersites. Let me carry another to his horse, for
that's the more capable creature.

Achilles. My mind is troubled like a fountain
stirr'd,   310
And I myself see not the bottom of it.

Thersites. Would the fountain of your mind were
clear again, that I might water an ass at it. I had
rather be a tick in a sheep than such a valiant ignorance.   [*Exeunt.*]

305 **catlings** catgut strings for musical instruments. 309 **capable**
intelligent.

Act IV

SCENE 1

Enter at one door Aeneas with a torch; at another Paris, Deiphobus, Antenor, Diomed the Grecian, with torches.

Paris. See, ho! Who is that there?
Deiphobus.   It is the Lord Aeneas.
Aeneas. Is the prince there in person?
Had I so good occasion to lie long
As you, Prince Paris, nothing but heavenly business
Should rob my bedmate of my company.   5
Diomedes. That's my mind too. Good morrow, Lord
          Aeneas.
Paris. A valiant Greek, Aeneas; take his hand.
Witness the process of your speech, [wherein]
You told how Diomed in a whole week by days   9
Did haunt you in the field.
Aeneas.   Health to you, valiant sir,
During all question of the gentle truce;
But when I meet you arm'd, as black defiance
As heart can think or courage execute!
Diomedes. The one and other Diomed embraces.
Our bloods are now in calm, and so long, health.   15
But when contention and occasion meets,
By Jove, I'll play the hunter for thy life
With all my force, pursuit, and policy.
Aeneas. And thou shalt hunt a lion that will fly

8 **process** course, gist. 8 **wherein** F *within.* 9 **by days** day by day.
11 **question** discussion.

85

With his face backward. In humane gentleness,   20
Welcome to Troy; now, by Anchises' life,
Welcome indeed. By Venus' hand I swear,
No man alive can love in such a sort
The thing he means to kill more excellently.   24
 Diomedes. We sympathize. Jove let Aeneas live,
If to my sword his fate be not the glory,
A thousand complete courses of the sun,
But in mine emulous honor let him die,
With every joint a wound, and that tomorrow.
 Aeneas. We know each other well.   30
 Diomedes. We do, and long to know each other
  worse.
 Paris. This is the most despiteful'st gentle greeting,
The noblest hateful love that ere I heard of.
What business, lord, so early?
 Aeneas. I was sent for to the king, but why, I know
  not.   35
 Paris. His purpose meets you. It was to bring this
  Greek
To Calchas' house, and there to render him,
For the enfree'd Antenor, the fair Cressid.
Let's have your company; or if you please
Haste there before us. I constantly do think,   40
Or rather call my thought a certain knowledge,
My brother Troilus lodges there tonight.
Rouse him and give him note of our approach,
With the whole quality whereof. I fear   44
We shall be much unwelcome.

21 **Anchises'** Anchises was Aeneas' father. 22 **Venus'** Venus was
Aeneas' mother. 25 **sympathize** agree, are of the same mind.
27 **complete** stressed ´ —. 28 **emulous** envious. 36 **His purpose
meets you** his reason is right here before you. 40 **constantly** con-
fidently. 44 **quality** substance, occasion of the visit.

Aeneas.　　　　　　　　　　That I assure you.
Troilus had rather Troy were borne to Greece
Than Cressid borne from Troy.
　Paris.　　　　　　　　　　There is no help.
The bitter disposition of the time
Will have it so. On, lord, we'll follow you.　　49
　Aeneas. Good morrow, all.　　　*Exit Aeneas.*
　Paris. And tell me, noble Diomed; faith, tell me
　　true,
Even in the soul of sound good fellowship,
Who in your thoughts merits fair Helen most,
Myself or Menelaus?
　Diomedes.　　　　Both alike.
He merits well to have her that doth seek her,　　55
Not making any scruple of her soilure,
With such a hell of pain and world of charge.
And you as well to keep her that defend her,
Not palating the taste of her dishonor,
With such a costly loss of wealth and friends.　　60
He, like a puling cuckold, would drink up
The lees and dregs of a flat tamed piece.
You, like a lecher, out of whorish loins
Are pleas'd to breed out your inheritors.　　64
Both merits pois'd, each weighs nor less nor more,
But he as he; which heavier for a whore?
　Paris. You are too bitter to your countrywoman.
　Diomedes. She's bitter to her country. Hear me,
　　Paris.
For every false drop in her bawdy veins

56 **soilure** soiled state, dishonor. 57 **charge** trouble expense. 62
tamed opened, with seal broken (with senses pointing both ways
in the pun on *piece*). **piece** cask of wine; also a slang term for a
woman. 65 **pois'd** weighed. 65 **nor less** F *no lesse*. 66 **which . . .
whore?** N.

A Grecian's life hath sunk; for every scruple   70
Of her contaminated carrion weight
A Troyan hath been slain. Since she could speak,
She hath not given so many good words breath
As for her Greeks and Troyans suff'red death.
  Paris. Fair Diomed, you do as chapmen do,   75
Dispraise the thing that you desire to buy;
But we in silence hold this virtue well;
We'll not commend what we intend to sell.
Here lies our way.   *Exeunt.*

SCENE 2

Enter Troilus and Cressida.

  Troilus. Dear, trouble not yourself. The morn is
    cold.
  Cressida. Then, sweet my lord, I'll call mine uncle
    down.
He shall unbolt the gates.
  Troilus.   Trouble him not.
To bed, to bed. Sleep kill those pretty eyes,
And give as soft attachment to thy senses   5
As infants empty of all thought.
  Cressida.   Good morrow, then.
  Troilus. I prithee now, to bed.
  Cressida.   Are you aweary of me?
  Troilus. O Cressida! But that the busy day,
Wak'd by the lark, hath rous'd the ribald crows,
And dreaming night will hide our eyes no longer,   10
I would not from thee.

70 **scruple** a very small unit of weight. 75 **chapmen** petty merchants. 78 **We'll . . . sell** N. 4 **kill** overpower, subdue. 8 **But that** except that.

Cressida. Night hath been too brief.

Troilus. Beshrew the witch! With venomous wights
    she stays
As [tediously] as hell, but flies the grasps of love
With wings more momentary swift than thought.
You will catch cold, and curse me.   15

Cressida. Prithee, tarry. You men will never tarry.
O foolish Cressid, I might have still held off,
And then you would have tarried. Hark, there's one
    up?

Pandarus. Within. What's all the doors open here?

Troilus. It is your uncle.   *Enter Pandarus.*

Cressida. A pestilence on him. Now will he be mocking. I shall have such a life!   22

Pandarus. How now, how now? How go maiden-
heads? Hear you, maid, where's my cousin Cressid?

Cressida. Go hang yourself, you naughty mocking
    uncle!   26
You bring me to do—and then you flout me too.

Pandarus. To do what? To do what? Let her say
what! What have I brought you to do?

Cressida. Come, come, beshrew your heart. You'll
nere be good, nor suffer others.   30

Pandarus. Ha, ha! Alas, poor wretch. A poor chipochia, hast not slept tonight? Would he not, a
naughty man, let it sleep? A bugbear take him!
                  One knocks.

Cressida. Did not I tell you? Would he were
    knock'd i' th' head!
Who's that at door? Good uncle, go and see.   35
My lord, come you again into my chamber.
You smile and mock me, as if I meant naughtily.

Troilus. Ha, ha.

12 **venomous wights** evil creatures. 13 **tediously** F **hidiously**
31–2 **chipochia** N.

Cressida. Come, you are deceiv'd; I think of no
    such thing.
How earnestly they knock! Pray you, come in.   40
                    Knock.
I would not for half Troy have you seen here.
                    Exeunt.
Pandarus. Who's there? What's the matter? Will
you beat down the door? How now, what's the mat-
ter?

[*Enter Aeneas.*]

Aeneas. Good morrow, lord, good morrow.   45
Pandarus. Who's there? My Lord Aeneas? By my
troth, I knew you not. What news with you so early?
Aeneas. Is not Prince Troilus here?
Pandarus. Here? What should he do here?   49
Aeneas. Come, he is here, my lord; do not deny him.
It doth import him much to speak with me.
Pandarus. Is he here, say you? 'Tis more than I
know, I'll be sworn. For my own part, I came in late.
What should he do here?   54
Aeneas. Who! Nay then. Come, come, you'll do him
wrong ere y' are ware. You'll be so true to him to
be false to him. Do not you know of him, but yet go
fetch him hither; go.   [*Exit Pandarus.*]

Enter Troilus.

Troilus. How now! What's the matter?
Aeneas. My lord, I scarce have leisure to salute
    you,   60
My matter is so rash. There is at hand
Paris, your brother, and Deiphobus,

51 **doth import him much** is very important to him. 61 **rash**
urgent.

90

The Grecian Diomed, and our Antenor
Deliver'd to us; and for him forthwith,
Ere the first sacrifice, within this hour,   65
We must give up to Diomedes' hand
The Lady Cressida.

Troilus.   Is it concluded so?

Aeneas. By Priam and the general state of Troy.
They are at hand and ready to effect it.

Troilus. How my achievements mock me!   70
I will go meet them. And my Lord Aeneas,
We met by chance; you did not find me here.

Aeneas. Good, good, my lord. The secrets of nature
Have not more gift in taciturnity.   *Exeunt.*

Enter Pandarus and Cressid.

Pandarus. Is't possible? No sooner got but lost!
The divel take Antenor! The young prince will go
mad. A plague upon Antenor! I would they had
broke's neck!

Cressida. How now? What's the matter? Who was
here?   80

Pandarus. Ah, ha!

Cressida. Why sigh you so profoundly? Where's
     my lord? Gone?
Tell me, sweet uncle, what's the matter?

Pandarus. Would I were as deep under the earth
as I am above!   86

Cressida. O, the gods! What's the matter?

Pandarus. Prithee, get thee in. Would thou hadst
nere been born; I knew thou wouldst be his death. O
poor gentleman! A plague upon Antenor!   90

66 **Diomedes'** F *Diomeds*. **73 secrets** possibly three syllables here.

91

Cressida. Good uncle, I beseech you, on my knees I
beseech you, what's the matter?

Pandarus. Thou must be gone, wench, thou must be
gone. Thou art chang'd for Antenor. Thou must to
thy father, and be gone from Troilus. 'Twill be his
death; 'twill be his bane. He cannot bear it.   96

Cressida. O, you immortal gods! I will not go.

Pandarus. Thou must.

Cressida. I will not, uncle! I have forgot my father;
I know no touch of consanguinity;   100
No kin, no love, no blood, no soul, so near me
As the sweet Troilus. O, you gods divine!
Make Cressid's name the very crown of falsehood
If ever she leave Troilus! Time, force, and death
Do to this body what extremity you can,   105
But the strong base and building of my love
Is as the very center of the earth,
Drawing all things to it. I will go in and weep.

Pandarus. Do, do.

Cressida. Tear my bright hair, and scratch my
      praised cheeks,   110
Crack my clear voice with sobs, and break my heart
With sounding Troilus. I will not go from Troy.

                                        Exeunt.

SCENE 3

*Enter Paris, Troilus, Aeneas, Deiphobus,
Antenor, and Diomedes.*

Paris. It is great morning, and the hour prefix'd
Of her delivery to this valiant Greek

94 **chang'd** exchanged. 96 **bane** destruction, death. 1 **great morning** full daylight. 2 **delivery** read 'deliv'ry.'

Comes fast upon. Good my brother Troilus,
Tell you the lady what she is to do,   4
And haste her to the purpose.
    Troilus.   Walk into her house.
I'll bring her to the Grecian presently;
And to his hand when I deliver her,
Think it an altar and thy brother Troilus
A priest, there off'ring to it his [own] heart.
    Paris. I know what 'tis to love,   10
And would, as I shall pity, I could help.
Please you walk in, my lords.   *Exeunt.*

SCENE 4

Enter Pandarus and Cressid.

    Pandarus. Be moderate, be moderate.
    Cressida. Why tell you me of moderation?
The grief is fine, full perfect that I taste,
And [violenteth] in a sense as strong
As that which causeth it. How can I moderate it? 5
If I could temporize with my affection
Or brew it to a weak and colder palate,
The like allayment could I give my grief.
My love admits no qualifying [dross];

Enter Troilus.

No more my grief, in such a precious loss.   10
    Pandarus. Here, here, here he comes, a sweet duck.
    Cressida. O Troilus! Troilus!
    Pandarus. What a pair of spectacles is here! Let
me embrace too. 'O heart,' as the goodly saying is,

---

9 **his own heart** F *his heart.* 4 **violenteth** rages violently; F *no lesse.* 9 **dross** impurity; F *cross.*

> *O heart, heavy heart*   **15**
> *Why sighest thou without breaking?*

Where he answers again,

> *Because thou canst not ease thy smart*
> *By friendship nor by speaking.*   **19**

There was never a truer rhyme. Let us cast away
nothing, for we may live to have need of such a verse.
We see it, we see it. How now, lambs?
  Troilus. Cressid, I love thee in so strange a purity
That the bless'd gods, as angry with my fancy,
More bright in zeal than the devotion which   **25**
Cold lips blow to their deities, take thee from me.
  Cressida. Have the gods envy?
  Pandarus. Ay, ay, ay, ay. 'Tis too plain a case.
  Cressida. And is it true that I must go from Troy?
  Troilus. A hateful truth!
  Cressida.   What, and from Troilus too?
  Troilus. From Troy, and Troilus.
  Cressida.   Is't possible? **31**
  Troilus. And suddenly, where injury of chance
Puts back leave-taking, justles roughly by
All time of pause, rudely beguiles our lips
Of all rejoindure, forcibly prevents   **35**
Our lock'd embrasures, strangles our dear vows,
Even in the birth of our own laboring breath.
We two, that with so many thousand sighs
Did buy each other, must poorly sell ourselves
With the rude brevity and discharge of [one].   **40**
Injurious time now with a robber's haste

---

24 **fancy** love. 32 **injury of chance** fortuitous ill treatment. 35 **rejoindure** reunion N. 36 **embrasures** embraces. 40 **one** F *our*.

Crams his rich thiev'ry up, he knows not how.
As many farewells as be stars in heaven,
With distinct breath, and consign'd kisses to them,
He fumbles up into a loose adieu,   45
And scants us with a single famish'd kiss,
Distasting with the salt of broken tears.
   Aeneas. *Within.* My lord, is the lady ready?
   Troilus. Hark, you are call'd. Some say the genius
    so
Cries 'Come!' to him that instantly must die.   50
Bid them have patience; she shall come anon.
   Pandarus. Where are my tears? Rain, to lay this
    wind,
Or my heart will be blown up by the root.   [*Exit.*]
   Cressida. I must then to the Grecians?
   Troilus.   No remedy.
   Cressida. A woeful Cressid 'mongst the merry
    Greeks.   55
When shall we see again?
   Troilus.   Hear me, my love;
Be thou but true of heart—
   Cressida. I, true! How now? What wicked deem is
    this?
   Troilus. Nay, we must use expostulation kindly,
For it is parting from us.   60
I speak not 'Be thou true' as fearing thee,
For I will throw my glove to death himself
That there's no maculation in thy heart;
But 'Be thou true' say I to fashion in

42 **thiev'ry** F *theiverie.* 44 **distinct . . . consign'd** both stressed
⌣́ —. 47 **Distasting** destroying the taste. **tears** N. 49 **genius** N.
52 **wind** i.e. of sighs. 56 **When . . . again** N. 58 **deem** surmise,
supposition. 63 **maculation** stain.

My sequent protestation. Be thou true,   65
And I will see thee.

    Cressida.   O, you shall be expos'd,
My lord, to dangers as infinite as imminent.
But I'll be true.

    Troilus.   And I'll grow friend with danger.
Wear this sleeve.

    Cressida.   And you this glove.
When shall I see you?   70

    Troilus. I will corrupt the Grecian sentinels,
To give thee nightly visitation.
But yet be true.

    Cressida.   O heavens! 'Be true' again?

    Troilus. Hear why I speak it, love.
The Grecian youths are full of quality;   75
Their loving well compos'd with gift of nature,
[Flowing] and swelling ore with arts and exercise.
How novelties may move, and parts with person,
Alas, a kind of godly jealously,
Which I beseech you call a virtuous sin,   80
Makes me afraid.

    Cressida.   O heavens! You love me not!

    Troilus. Die I a villain then!
In this I do not call your faith in question
So mainly as my merit. I cannot sing,
Nor heel the high lavolt, nor sweeten talk,   85
Nor play at subtle games—fair virtues all,
To which the Grecians are most prompt and preg-
    nant.
But I can tell that in each grace of these

---

75 quality natural gifts. 77 Flowing F *flawing* N. 78 parts with
person accomplishments with personal charm. 84 mainly much.
85 lavolt a lively Italian dance. 87 pregnant ready.

There lurks a still and dumb-discoursive divel   89
That tempts most cunningly. But be not tempted!
  Cressida. Do you think I will?
  Troilus.   **No,**
But something may be done that we will not,
And sometimes we are divels to ourselves,
When we will tempt the frailty of our powers,
Presuming on their changeful potency.   95
  Aeneas. Within. Nay, good my lord?
  Troilus.   Come, kiss and let us part.
  Paris. Within. Brother Troilus?
  Troilus.   Good brother, come you hither
And bring Aeneas and the Grecian with you.
  Cressida. My lord, will you be true?
  Troilus. Who, I? Alas, it is my vice, my fault.   100
Whiles others fish with craft for great opinion,
I with great truth catch mere simplicity;
Whilst some with cunning gild their copper crowns,
With truth and plainness I do wear mine bare.

    Enter [*Paris, Aeneas, Deiphobus, Antenor,*
             and Diomed.]

Fear not my truth. The moral of my wit   105
Is plain and true; there's all the reach of it.
Welcome, Sir Diomed; here is the lady,
Which for Antenor we deliver you.
At the port, lord, I'll give her to thy hand,
And by the way possess thee what she is.   110
Entreat her fair; and by my soul, fair Greek,
If ere thou stand at mercy of my sword,

89 **dumb-discoursive** silent-speaking. 99 **true** F has a superfluous
Exit after this word. 101 **craft** craftiness, cunning. SD **Paris,
Aeneas** . . . N. 109 **port** gate. 110 **possess** inform. 111 **Entreat**
treat.

Name Cressid and thy life shall be as safe
As Priam is in Ilion.

Diomedes.   Fair Lady Cressid,   114
So please you, save the thanks this prince expects.
The lustre in your eye, heaven in your cheek,
Pleads your fair [usage], and to Diomed
You shall be mistress and command him wholly.

Troilus. Grecian, thou dost not use me courteously,
To shame the zeal of my petition to thee   120
In praising her. I tell thee, lord of Greece,
She is as far high soaring ore thy praises
As thou unworthy to be call'd her servant.
I charge thee use her well, even for my charge,
For by the dreadful Pluto, if thou dost not,   125
Though the great bulk Achilles be thy guard,
I'll cut thy throat.

Diomedes.   O, be not mov'd, Prince Troilus.
Let me be privileg'd by my place and message
To be a speaker free. When I am hence,
I'll answer to my lust. And know, my lord,   130
I'll nothing do on charge. To her own worth
She shall be priz'd; but that you say, 'Be't so,'
I'll speak it in my spirit and honor, 'No.'

Troilus. Come, to the port. I'll tell thee, Diomed,
This brave shall oft make thee to hide thy head.   135
Lady, give me your hand; and as we walk
To our own selves bend we our needful talk.

Sound trumpet.

Paris. Hark, Hector's trumpet!

Aeneas.   How have we spent this morning!

117 usage F *visage.* 120 zeal . . . thee N. 124 for my charge at
my command or exhortation. 130 lust inclinations. 131 charge
compulsion. 132 but that but simply because. 135 brave defiance,
dare.

The prince must think me tardy and remiss
That swore to ride before him in the field.   140
    Paris. 'Tis Troilus' fault. Come, come, to field with
        him.
        Exeunt [Troilus, Cressida, Diomed, and Paris].
    Deiphobus. Let us make ready straight.
    Aeneas. Yea, with a bridegroom's fresh alacrity
Let us address to tend on Hector's heels.
The glory of our Troy doth this day lie   145
On his fair worth and single chivalry.   *[Exeunt.]*

SCENE 5

Enter Ajax, armed, Achilles, Patroclus,
Agamemnon, Menelaus, Ulysses, Nestor,
Calchas, etc.

    Agamemnon. Here art thou in appointment fresh
        and fair,
Anticipating time. With starting courage,
Give with thy trumpet a loud note to Troy,
Thou dreadful Ajax, that the appalled air
May pierce the head of the great combatant   5
And hale him hither.
    Ajax.   Thou trumpet, there's my purse;
Now crack thy lungs, and split thy brazen pipe!
Blow, villain, till thy sphered bias cheek
Outswell the colic of puff'd Aquilon.
Come, stretch thy chest and let thy eyes spout
        blood;   10

142 **Let . . . straight** N. 144 **address** make ready. SD **Calchas** N.
1 **appointment** equipment. 2 **starting** bounding, energetic. 6 **purse**
i.e. of the lips. 8 **bias** puffed out. 9 **Aquilon** the north wind.

Thou blowest for Hector.

Ulysses. No trumpet answers.

Achilles. 'Tis but early days.

Agamemnon. Is not [yond] Diomed with Calchas' daughter?

[*Enter Diomed and Cressida.*]

Ulysses. 'Tis he. I ken the manner of his gait;
He rises on the toe. That spirit of his   15
In aspiration lifts him from the earth.

Agamemnon. Is this the Lady Cressid?

Diomedes. Even she.

Agamemnon. Most dearly welcome to the Greeks, sweet lady.

Nestor. Our general doth salute you with a kiss.

Ulysses. Yet is the kindness but particular;   20
'Twere better she were kiss'd in general.

Nestor. And very courtly counsel. I'll begin.
So much for Nestor.

Achilles. I'll take that winter from your lips, fair lady.
Achilles bids you welcome.   25

Menelaus. I had good argument for kissing once.

Patroclus. But that's no argument for kissing now.
For thus popp'd Paris in his hardiment
And parted thus you and your argument.   29

Ulysses. O deadly gall, and theme of all our scorns,
For which we lose our heads, to gild his horns.

Patroclus. The first was Menelaus' kiss, this mine;
Patroclus kisses you.

Menelaus. O, this is trim!

Patroclus. Paris and I kiss evermore for him.

12 days in the day. 13 yond F *yong.* 28 hardiment audacity. 29
And . . . argument N. 31 horns i.e. cuckold's horns.

Menelaus. I'll have my kiss, sir. Lady, by your
    leave.   35

Cressida. In kissing do you render or receive?

Patroclus. Both take and give.

Cressida.   I'll make my match to live,

The kiss you take is better than you give.

Therefore no kiss.

Menelaus. I'll give you boot. I'll give you three for
    one.   40

Cressida. You are an odd man. Give even or give
    none.

Menelaus. An odd man, lady? Every man is odd.

Cressida. No, Paris is not; for you know 'tis true

That you are odd, and he is even with you.   44

Menelaus. You fillip me o' th' head.

Cressida.   No, I'll be sworn.

Ulysses. It were no match, your nail against his
    horn.

May I, sweet lady, beg a kiss of you?

Cressida. You may.

Ulysses.   I do desire it.

Cressida.   Why beg then?

Ulysses. Why then, for Venus' sake, give me a kiss

When Helen is a maid again, and his.   50

Cressida. I am your debtor. Claim it when 'tis due.

Ulysses. Never's my day, and then a kiss of you.

Diomedes. Lady, a word. I'll bring you to your
    father.   [*Exeunt Diomed and Cressida.*]

Nestor. A woman of quick sense.

Ulysses.   Fie, fie upon her!

37 **make . . . live** bet my life. 40 **boot** to boot, extra advantages.
45 **fillip** hit (a reference to his cuckold's horns). 50 **his** i.e.
Menelaus'. 54 **sense** pun on two meanings: 'intelligence' and
'sensuality.'

There's a language in her eye, her cheek, her lip;   55
Nay, her foot speaks. Her wanton spirits look out
At every joint and motive of her body.
O, these encounterers so glib of tongue,
That give a coasting welcome [ere] it comes,
And wide unclasp the tables of their thoughts   60
To every tickling reader! Set them down
For sluttish spoils of opportunity,
And daughters of the game.

   Enter all of Troy: Hector, Paris, Aeneas,
    Helenus, and attendants. Flourish.

 All. The Troyans' trumpet.
 Agamemnon.   Yonder comes the troop.
 Aeneas. Hail, all you state of Greece. What shall be
   done   65
To him that victory commands? Or do you purpose
A victor shall be known? Will you the knights
Shall to the edge of all extremity
Pursue each other, or shall be divided
By any voice or order of the field?   70
Hector bade ask.
 Agamemnon. Which way would Hector have it?
 Aeneas. He cares not. He'll obey conditions.
 Agamemnon. 'Tis done like Hector; but securely
   done,
A little proudly, and great deal disprizing
The knight oppos'd.
 Aeneas.   If not Achilles, sir,   75

---

57 **motive** unit, part that produces motion. 58 **encounterers** flirts, 'forward' women. 59 **a coasting** N. **ere** F *ete*. 60 **tables** tablets. 61 **tickling** avid, curious. 63 **game** N. 67 **Will you** do you wish. 72 **conditions** four syllables here. 74 **disprizing** depreciating; Q *misprising.*

  102

What is your name?

Achilles.   If not Achilles, nothing.

Aeneas. Therefore, Achilles. But what ere, know
     this:

In the extremity of great and little,

Valor and pride excel themselves in Hector;

The one almost as infinite as all,   80

The other blank as nothing. Weigh him well,.

And that which looks like pride is courtesy.

This Ajax is half made of Hector's blood,

In love whereof, half Hector stays at home;

Half heart, half hand, half Hector comes to seek   85

This blended knight, half Troyan and half Greek.

Achilles. A maiden battle then? O, I perceive you.

[*Enter Diomedes.*]

Agamemnon. Here is Sir Diomed. Go, gentle knight;

Stand by our Ajax. As you and Lord Aeneas

Consent upon the order of their fight,   90

So be it, either to the uttermost

Or else a [breath]. The combatants being kin

Half stints their strife before their strokes begin.

Ulysses. They are oppos'd already.

Agamemnon. What Troyan is that same that looks
     so heavy?   95

Ulysses. The youngest son of Priam, a true knight,

Not yet mature yet matchless, firm of word,

Speaking in deeds and deedless in his tongue;

Not soon provok'd, nor being provok'd, soon calm'd.

His heart and hand both open and both free;   100

For what he has, he gives; what thinks, he shews;

---

83 **Ajax . . . blood** N. 87 **maiden battle** a draw, an issueless
combat. 92 **breath** breathing space; F *breach.* 96 **knight** N. 100
free generous, noble.

Yet gives he not till judgment guide his bounty,
Nor dignifies an impair thought with breath;
Manly as Hector, but more dangerous,
For Hector in his blaze of wrath subscribes   105
To tender objects, but he, in heat of action,
Is more vindicative than jealous love.
They call him Troilus, and on him erect
A second hope as fairly built as Hector.
Thus says Aeneas, one that knows the youth,   110
Even to his inches, and with private soul
Did in great Ilion thus translate him to me.
                                        Alarum.

   Agamemnon. They are in action.
   Nestor. Now, Ajax, hold thine own.
   Troilus. Hector, thou sleep'st. Awake thee!   115
   Agamemnon. His blows are well dispos'd there,
Ajax.   *Trumpets cease.*
   Diomedes. You must no more.
   Aeneas. Princes, enough, so please you.
   Ajax. I am not warm yet. Let us fight again.   120
   Diomedes. As Hector pleases.
   Hector.   Why then will I no more.
Thou art, great lord, my father's sister's son,
A cousin german to great Priam's seed.
The obligation of our blood forbids
A gory emulation 'twixt us twain.   125
Were thy commixion Greek and Troyan so
That thou couldst say, 'This hand is Grecian all
And this is Troyan, the sinews of this leg
All Greek, and this all Troy; my mother's blood

---

103 **impair** unsuitable, unconsidered(stressed $\underline{}$ —). 107 **vindicative** vindictive. 111 **to his inches** his exact height, i.e. very
intimately. **with private soul** in confidence. 112 **translate** reveal,
interpret. 125 **emulation** rivalry. 126 **commixion** mixture.

Runs on the dexter cheek, and this sinister   130
Bounds in my father's,' by Jove multipotent,
Thou shouldst not bear from me a Greekish member
Wherein my sword had not impressure made
Of our rank feud. But the just gods gainsay   134
That any drop thou borrow'dst from thy mother,
My sacred aunt, should by my mortal sword
Be drained. Let me embrace thee, Ajax.
By him that thunders, thou hast lusty arms!
Hector would have them fall upon him thus.
Cousin, all honor to thee.

   Ajax.   I thank thee, Hector.   140
Thou art too gentle and too free a man.
I came to kill thee, cousin, and bear hence
A great addition earned in thy death.

   Hector. Not Neoptolymus so mirable,   144
On whose bright crest fame with her loud'st oyes
Cries, 'This is he,' [could] promise to himself
A thought of added honor torn from Hector.

   Aeneas. There is expectance here from both the
    sides
What further you will do.

   Hector.   We'll answer it;
The issue is embracement. Ajax, farewell.   150

   Ajax. If I might in entreaties find success,
As seld I have the chance, I would desire
My famous cousin to our Grecian tents.

   Diomedes. 'Tis Agamemnon's wish, and great Achil-
    les

130 **dexter** right. **sinister** left (stressed — ′ —). 131 **multipotent**
very powerful. 134 **gainsay** forbid. 141 **free** generous, noble. 144
Neoptolymus N. **mirable** admirable, marvelous. 145 **oyes** N. 146
could F *could'st.* 148 **expectance** expectation, wondering. 150
issue result. 152 **seld** seldom. **desire** invite.

Doth long to see unarm'd the valiant Hector. 155

   Hector. Aeneas, call my brother Troilus to me,
And signify this loving interview
To the expecters of our Troyan part.
Desire them home. Give me thy hand, my cousin;
I will go eat with thee and see your knights. 160

Enter Agamemnon and the rest.

   Ajax. Great Agamemnon comes to meet us here.
   Hector. The worthiest of them tell me name by
     name;
But for Achilles, mine own searching eyes
Shall find him by his large and portly size. 164
   Agamemnon. Worthy of arms, as welcome as to one
That would be rid of such an enemy.
But that's no welcome. Understand more clear;
What's past and what's to come is strew'd with
     husks
And formless ruin of oblivion;
But in this extant moment, faith and troth, 170
Strain'd purely, from all hollow bias drawing,
Bids thee with most divine integrity
From heart of very heart, great Hector, welcome.
   Hector. I thank thee, most imperious Agamemnon.
   Agamemnon. My well-fam'd lord of Troy, no less to
     you. 175
   Menelaus. Let me confirm my princely brother's
     greeting.
You brace of warlike brothers, welcome hither.

158 **expecters . . . part** Trojans who are waiting. 159 **Desire them** request them to go. SD **Enter . . . rest** N. 164 **portly** majestic, imposing. 169 **oblivion** four distinct syllables here. 171 **from . . . drawing** withdrawing from bias; cf. I.3.15 N. 175 **My . . . you** probably addressed to Troilus.

Hector. Who must we answer?

Aeneas.   The noble Menelaus.

Hector. O, you, my lord! By Mars his gauntlet, thanks.

Mock not that I affect th' untraded oath;   180
Your quondam wife swears still by Venus' glove.
She's well, but bade me not commend her to you.

Menelaus. Name her not now, sir; she's a deadly theme.

Hector. O pardon! I offend.

Nestor. I have, thou gallant Troyan, seen thee oft,
Laboring for destiny, make cruel way   186
Through ranks of Greekish youth, and I have seen thee
As hot as Perseus, spur thy Phrygian steed,
And seen thee scorning forfeits and subduements
When thou hast hung thy advanced sword i' th' air,
Not letting it decline on the declin'd;   191
That I have said unto my standers-by,
'Lo, Jupiter is yonder, dealing life.'
And I have seen thee pause and take thy breath
When that a ring of Greeks have hemm'd thee in,
Like an Olympian wrestling. This have I seen,   196
But this thy countenance, still lock'd in steel,
I never saw till now. I knew thy grandsire
And once fought with him. He was a soldier good,
But by great Mars, the captain of us all,   200
Never like thee. Let an old man embrace thee,
And, worthy warrior, welcome to our tents.

Aeneas. 'Tis the old Nestor.

179 **Mars his gauntlet** Mars' gauntlet. 180 **untraded** unusual, not customary. 181 **quondam** former. 188 **Perseus** cf. I.3.42 gloss. 189 **subduements** situations in which opponent is subdued. 197 **still** continually. 198 **grandsire** N.

Hector. Let me embrace thee, good old chronicle,
That hast so long walk'd hand in hand with time.
Most reverend Nestor, I am glad to clasp thee. 206
  Nestor. I would my arms could match thee in con-
          tention
As they contend with thee in courtesy.
  Hector. I would they could.
  Nestor. Ha? By this white beard, I'ld fight with
          thee tomorrow. 210
Well, welcome, welcome. I have seen the time.
  Ulysses. I wonder now how yonder city stands,
When we have here her base and pillar by us.
  Hector. I know your favor, Lord Ulysses, well.
Ah sir, there's many a Greek and Troyan dead 215
Since first I saw yourself and Diomed
In Ilion on your Greekish embassy.
  Ulysses. Sir, I foretold you then what would ensue.
My prophecy is but half his journey yet,
For yonder walls that pertly front your town, 220
Yond towers, whose wanton tops do buss the clouds,
Must kiss their own feet.
  Hector.   I must not believe you.
There they stand yet. And modestly I think,
The fall of every Phrygian stone will cost
A drop of Grecian blood. The end crowns all, 225
And that old common arbitrator, Time,
Will one day end it.
  Ulysses.   So to him we leave it.
Most gentle and most valiant Hector, welcome.
After the general, I beseech you next
To feast with me and see me at my tent. 230

204 **chronicle** history book (here used figuratively). 219 **favor**
face, aspect. 220 **pertly** boldly. 221 **buss** kiss. 223 **modestly**
without exaggeration.

Achilles. I shall forestall thee, Lord Ulysses, thou.
Now Hector I have fed mine eyes on thee;
I have with exact view perus'd thee, Hector,
And quoted joint by joint.

 Hector.   Is this Achilles?

 Achilles. I am Achilles.   235

 Hector. Stand fair, I prithee; let me look on thee.

 Achilles. Behold thy fill.

 Hector.   Nay, I have done already.

 Achilles. Thou art too brief. I will the second time,
As I would buy thee, view thee limb by limb. 239

 Hector. O, like a book of sport thou'lt read me ore;
But there's more in me than thou understandst.
Why dost thou so oppress me with thine eye?

 Achilles. Tell me, you heavens, in which part of his
  body
Shall I destroy him? Whether there, or there, or
  there,
That I may give the local wound a name, 245
And make distinct the very breach whereout
Hector's great spirit flew. Answer me, heavens.

 Hector. It would discredit the bless'd gods, proud
  man,
To answer such a question. Stand again.
Think'st thou to catch my life so pleasantly 250
As to prenominate in nice conjecture
Where thou wilt hit me dead?

 Achilles.   I tell thee, yea.

 Hector. Wert thou the oracle to tell me so,
I'd not believe thee. Henceforth guard thee well,
For I'll not kill thee there, nor there, nor there, 255

233 **exact** here stressed $\overset{\prime}{-}$ —. 234 **quoted** scrutinized. 251 **prenominate** specify or name beforehand. **nice** precise.

But by the forge that stithied Mars his helm,
I'll kill thee everywhere, yea, ore and ore!
You wisest Grecians, pardon me this brag.
His insolence draws folly from my lips,
But I'll endeavor deeds to match these words,   260
Or may I never—
  Ajax.   Do not chafe thee, cousin.
And you, Achilles, let these threats alone,
Till accident or purpose bring you to't.
You may [have] every day enough of Hector
If you have stomach. The general state, I fear,   265
Can scarce entreat you to be odd with him.
  Hector. I pray you, let us see you in the field.
We have had pelting wars since you refus'd
The Grecians' cause.
  Achilles.   Dost thou entreat me, Hector?
Tomorrow do I meet thee fell as death;   270
Tonight, all friends.
  Hector.   Thy hand upon that match!
  Agamemnon. First, all you peers of Greece, go to
    my tent;
There in the full convive you. Afterwards,
As Hector's leisure and your bounties shall
Concur together, severally entreat him.   275
Beat loud the taborins, let the trumpets blow,
That this great soldier may his welcome know.
            Exeunt [*all but Troilus and Ulysses*].
  Troilus. My Lord Ulysses, tell me, I beseech you,
In what place of the field doth Calchas keep?   279

256 **stithied** forged. 261 **chafe thee** arouse yourself. 264 **may have**
F *may.* 266 **odd** at odds. 268 **pelting** petty, insignificant. 270 **fell**
fierce, cruel. 273 **convive you** be convivial, feast. 275 **severally**
entreat him individually invite (treat) him. 276 **taborins** drums.

Ulysses. At Menelaus' tent, most princely Troilus.
There Diomed doth feast with him tonight,
Who neither looks on heaven nor on earth,
But gives all gaze and bent of amorous view
On the fair Cressid.

    Troilus. Shall I, sweet lord, be bound to thee so
       much,   285
After we part from Agamemnon's tent,
To bring me thither?

    Ulysses.   You shall command me, sir.
As gentle tell me, of what honor was
This Cressida in Troy? Had she no lover there
That wails her absence?   290

    Troilus. O sir, to such as boasting shew their scars
A mock is due. Will you walk on, my lord?
She was belov'd, she lov'd; she is, and doth;
But still sweet love is food for Fortune's tooth.

                          Exeunt.

293 doth N.

Act V

SCENE 1

Enter Achilles and Patroclus.

Achilles. I'll heat his blood with Greekish wine to-
night,
Which with my scimitar I'll cool tomorrow.
Patroclus, let us feast him to the height.
Patroclus. Here comes Thersites.

Enter Thersites.

Achilles.   How now, thou core of envy?
Thou crusty batch of nature, what's the news?   5

Thersites. Why, thou picture of what thou seem'st,
and idol of idiot-worshipers, here's a letter for thee.

Achilles. From whence, fragment?

Thersites. Why, thou full dish of fool, from Troy.

Patroclus. Who keeps the tent now?   10

Thersites. The surgeon's box, or the patient's
wound.

Patroclus. Well said, adversity, and what need
these tricks?   14

Thersites. Prithee be silent, boy. I profit not by thy
talk. Thou art thought to be Achilles' male varlot.

Patroclus. Male varlot, you rogue? What's that?

Thersites. Why, his masculine whore. Now the rotten diseases of the South, guts-griping ruptures,
catarrhs, loads of gravel i' th' back, lethargies, cold

11 **surgeon's box** N. 16 **varlot** N. 20 **loads . . . back** kidney
stones. 20 **lethargies** apoplexies.
112

palsies, and the like take and take again such pre-
postrous discoveries!   22

Patroclus. Why, thou damnable box of envy, thou,
what meanst thou to curse thus?

Thersites. Do I curse thee?

Patroclus. Why no, you ruinous butt! You whoreson indistinguishable cur!   27

Thersites. No? Why art thou then exasperate,
thou idle, immaterial skein of sleyd silk? Thou green
sarcenet flap for a sore eye, thou tassel of a prodi-
gal's purse, thou! Ah, how the poor world is pest'red
with such water-flies, diminutives of nature!

Patroclus. Out, gall!

Thersites. Finch egg!   34

Achilles. My sweet Patroclus, I am thwarted quite
From my great purpose in tomorrow's battle.
Here is a letter from Queen Hecuba,
A token from her daughter, my fair love,
Both taxing me and gaging me to keep
An oath that I have sworn. I will not break it.   40
Fall Greeks, fail fame, honor or go or stay,
My major vow lies here; this I'll obey.
Come, come Thersites, help to trim my tent;
This night in banqueting must all be spent.   44
Away, Patroclus. [*Exeunt Achilles and Patroclus.*]

Thersites. With too much blood and too little brain,
these two may run mad; but if with too much brain
and too little blood they do, I'll be a curer of madmen. Here's Agamemnon, an honest fellow enough,

21 palsies N. 22 **discoveries** revelations. 26 **butt** cask of wine,
hogshead. 29 **immaterial** insignificant, flimsy. 29 **sleyd** raw, un-
twisted. 30 **sarcenet** fine silk. 39 **gaging** binding, engaging. 41
or . . . or either . . . or. SD **Exeunt . . . Patroclus** F has
merely *Exit.* Q has no SD.

and one that loves quails, but he has not so much brain as ear wax; and the goodly transformation of Jupiter there, his brother, the bull, the primitive statue and oblique memorial of cuckolds, a thrifty shoeing horn in a chain, hanging at his brother's leg —to what form but that he is, should wit larded with malice and malice forced with wit turn him to? To an ass were nothing; he is both ass and ox. To an ox were nothing; he is both ox and ass. To be a dog, a mule, a cat, a fitchew, a toad, a lizard, an owl, a puttock, or a herring without a roe, I would not care; but to be Menelaus, I would conspire against destiny. Ask me not what I would be, if I were not Thersites. For I care not to be the louse of a lazar, so I were not Menelaus. Hoy-day, spirits and fires!

Enter Hector, Ajax, Agamemnon, Ulysses,
Nestor, Diomed, with lights.

Agamemnon. We go wrong, we go wrong.
Ajax.   No, yonder 'tis.
There where we see the light.
Hector.   I trouble you.   66
Ajax. No, not a whit.

Enter Achilles.

Ulysses.   Here comes himself to guide you.
Achilles. Welcome, brave Hector. Welcome, princes all.
Agamemnon. So now, fair prince of Troy, I bid good night.   70

---

50 **quails** women, prostitutes. 51–3 **transformation** . . . **cuckolds** N. 54 **shoeing horn** shoe horn, tool N. 55 **that** that which. 56 **forced** stuffed, farced. 59 **fitchew** polecat. 60 **puttock** small hawk.

Ajax commands the guard to tend on you.

Hector. Thanks and good night to the Greeks' general.

Menelaus. Good night, my lord.

Hector. Good night, sweet Lord Menelaus.   75

Thersites. Sweet draught! 'Sweet,' quoth a? Sweet sink, sweet sewer!

Achilles. Good night and welcome, both at once, to those
That go or tarry.

Agamemnon.   Good night.   79

          [*Exeunt Agamemnon and Menelaus.*]

Achilles. Old Nestor tarries, and you too Diomed;
Keep Hector company an hour or two.

Diomedes. I cannot, lord. I have important business,
The tide whereof is now. Good night, great Hector.

Hector. Give me your hand.

Ulysses.   Follow his torch. He goes
To Calchas' tent. I'll keep you company.   85

Troilus. Sweet sir, you honor me.

Hector.   And so good night.

          [*Exeunt Diomed, Troilus, and Ulysses.*]

Achilles. Come, come, enter my tent.   87

          Exeunt [*Achilles, Hector, Ajax, and Nestor*].

Thersites. That same Diomed's a false-hearted rogue, a most unjust knave. I will no more trust him when he leers than I will a serpent when he hisses. He will spend his mouth and promise, like Brabbler the hound, but when he performs, astronomers foretell it, that it is prodigious—there will come some change. The sun borrows of the moon when Diomed

76 draught privy. 77 sink cesspool. SD F has no SD here. 83 tide time. SD Exeunt . . . Ulysses N. 91 Brabbler N.

115

keeps his word. I will rather leave to see Hector than not to dog him. They say he keeps a Troyan drab, and uses the traitor Calchas his tent. I'll after. Nothing but lechery! All incontinent varlots! [*Exit.*]

SCENE 2

Enter Diomed.

Diomedes. What, are you up here, ho? Speak.
Calchas. [*Within.*] Who calls?
Diomedes. Diomed. Calchas, I think, where's your daughter?
Calchas. [*Within.*] She comes to you.   5

Enter Troilus and Ulysses.

Ulysses. Stand where the torch may not discover us.

Enter Cressid.

Troilus. Cressid comes forth to him.
Diomedes. How now, my charge?   9
Cressida. Now, my sweet guardian, hark; a word with you.
Troilus. Yea, so familiar?
Ulysses. She will sing any man at first sight.
Thersites. And any man may [sing] her, if he can take her [cliff]; she's noted.   15
Diomedes. Will you remember?
Cressida. Remember? Yes.

95 leave to see leave off seeing. 97 Calchas his Calchas'; see II.1.54 N. after follow after. SD Exit F *Exeunt.* 6 discover reveal. 14 sing F *find.* 15 cliff clef, key; F *life.* 17 Cressida. Mistakenly labeled *Cal.* in both F and Q.

Diomedes. Nay, but do then; and let your mind be
coupled with your words.

Troilus. What should she remember? 20

Ulysses. List!

Cressida. Sweet honey Greek, tempt me no more to
folly.

Thersites. Roguery!

Diomedes. Nay, then— 25

Cressida. I'll tell you what.

Diomedes. Foh, foh! Come, tell a pin! You are a
forsworn—

Cressida. In faith, I cannot. What would you have
me do? 30

Thersites. A juggling trick, to be secretly open.

Diomedes. What did you swear you would bestow
on me?

Cressida. I prithee, do not hold me to mine oath.
Bid me do anything but that, sweet Greek.

Diomedes. Good night. 35

Troilus. Hold, patience.

Ulysses. How now, Troyan?

Cressida. Diomed.

Diomedes. No, no. Good night. I'll be your fool no
more. 40

Troilus. Thy better must.

Cressida. Hark, one word in your ear,

Troilus. O plague and madness!

Ulysses. You are moved, prince. Let us depart, I
pray you,
Lest your displeasure should enlarge itself
To wrathful terms. This place is dangerous; 45
The time right deadly. I beseech you go.

Troilus. Behold, I pray you.

27 tell a pin tell, nothing! **34 do anything** F *do not anything.*

Ulysses.   Nay, good my lord, go off.
You flow to great distraction. Come, my lord.

Troilus. I pray thee, stay.

Ulysses.   You have not patience; come.

Troilus. I pray you, stay. By hell and hell tor-
      ments,   50
I will not speak a word.

Diomedes.   And so good night.

Cressida. Nay, but you part in anger.

Troilus.   Doth that grieve thee?
O wither'd truth!

Ulysses.   Why, how now, lord?

Troilus.   By Jove,
I will be patient.

Cressida.   Guardian? Why, Greek!

Diomedes. Foh, foh! Adieu. You palter.   55

Cressida. In faith, I do not. Come hither once
      again.

Ulysses. You shake, my lord, at something. Will
      you go?
You will break out.

Troilus.   She strokes his cheek!

Ulysses.   Come, come.

Troilus. Nay, stay. By Jove, I will not speak a
      word!
There is between my will and all offenses   60
A guard of patience. Stay a little while.

Thersites. How the divel Luxury with his fat rump
and potato finger tickles these together. Fry, lechery, fry!

Diomedes. But will you, then?   65

Cressida. In faith, I will. Lo, never trust me else.

48 **flow** go toward.   55 **palter** equivocate, deal crookedly.   62
Luxury lechery.   63 **potato** N.

Diomedes. Give me some token for the surety of it.
Cressida. I'll fetch you one.   *Exit.*
Ulysses. You have sworn patience.
Troilus.   Fear me not, sweet lord.
I will not be myself, nor have cognition   70
Of what I feel. I am all patience.

Enter Cressid.

Thersites. Now, the pledge! Now, now, now!
Cressida. Here, Diomed; keep this sleeve.
Troilus. O beauty! Where is thy faith?
Ulysses. My lord.   75
Troilus. I will be patient; outwardly I will.
Cressida. You look upon that sleeve? Behold it well.
He lov'd me. O false wench! Give't me again.
Diomedes. Whose was't?
Cressida. It is no matter now I have't again.   80
I will not meet with you tomorrow night.
I prithee, Diomed, visit me no more.
Thersites. Now she sharpens. Well said, whetstone.
Diomedes. I shall have it.
Cressida.   What, this?
Diomedes.   Ay, that.
Cressida. O all you gods! O pretty, pretty pledge!
Thy master now lies thinking in his bed   86
Of thee and me, and sighs, and takes my glove,
And gives memorial dainty kisses to it,
As I kiss thee. Nay, do not snatch it from me.
He that takes that [doth take] my heart withal.   90
Diomedes. I had your heart before; this follows it.
Troilus. I did swear patience.

69 Fear me not you can depend on me. 89 **Nay . . . me** N.
90 **doth take** F *rakes;* F2 *takes.*

Cressida. You shall not have it, Diomed; faith, you
    shall not.
I'll give you something else.   94

Diomedes. I will have this. Whose was it?

Cressida.   It is no matter.

Diomedes. Come, tell me whose it was!

Cressida. 'Twas one that lov'd me better than you
    will.
But now you have it, take it.

Diomedes.   Whose was it?

Cressida. By all Diana's waiting women yond,
And by herself, I will not tell you whose.   100

Diomedes. Tomorrow will I wear it on my helm,
And grieve his spirit that dares not challenge it.

Troilus. Wert thou the divel and wor'st it on thy
    horn,
It should be challeng'd.

Cressida.   Well, well, 'tis done. 'Tis past;
And yet it is not. I will not keep my word.   105

Diomedes. Why then, farewell.
Thou never shalt mock Diomed again.

Cressida. You shall not go. One cannot speak a
    word
But it straight starts you.

Diomedes.   I do not like this fooling.

Thersites. Nor I, by Pluto! But that that likes not
me, pleases me best.   111

Diomedes. What, shall I come? The hour?

Cressida.   Ay, come. O Jove!
Do come. I shall be plagu'd.

Diomedes.   Farewell till then.   *Exit.*

99 **Diana's waiting women** the moon's attendants, the stars.
110–11 **likes not me** does not please me N. 113 **plagu'd** harassed
(perhaps in the sense of punishment).

Cressida. Good night. I prithee, come.

Troilus, farewell. One eye yet looks on thee,   115
But with my heart the other eye doth see.
Ah, poor our sex! This fault in us I find:
The error of our eye directs our mind.
What error leads must err. O then, conclude   119
Minds sway'd by eyes are full of turpitude.   *Exit.*

   Thersites. A proof of strength she could not pub-
     lish more;
Unless she say, 'My mind is now turn'd whore.'

   Ulysses. All's done, my lord.

   Troilus.   It is.

   Ulysses.   Why stay we then?

   Troilus. To make a recordation to my soul
Of every syllable that here was spoke.   125
But if I tell how these two did coact,
Shall I not lie in publishing a truth?
Sith yet there is a credence in my heart,
An esperance so obstinately strong
That doth invert that test of eyes and ears,   130
As if those organs had deceptious functions,
Created only to calumniate.
Was Cressid here?

   Ulysses.   I cannot conjure, Troyan.

   Troilus. She was not, sure.

   Ulysses.   Most sure she was.

   Troilus. Why, my negation hath no taste of mad-
     ness.   135

   Ulysses. Nor mine, my lord. Cressid was here but
     now.

   Troilus. Let it not be believ'd for womanhood!

124 **make a recordation** to make a record on, engrave on. 126
coact act together. 128 **Sith** since. 129 **esperance** hope. 130 **that
test** N. 131 **deceptious** deceptive.

Think we had mothers. Do not give advantage
To stubborn critics, apt without a theme
For depravation to square the general sex   140
By Cressid's rule. Rather think this not Cressid.
  Ulysses. What hath she done, prince, that can soil
    our mothers?
  Troilus. Nothing at all, unless that this were she.
  Thersites. Will he swagger himself out on's own
    eyes?   144
  Troilus. This she? No, this is Diomed's Cressida.
If beauty have a soul, this is not she;
If souls guide vows, if vows are sanctimony,
If sanctimony be the gods' delight,
If there be rule in unity itself,
This is not she. O madness of discourse!   150
That cause sets up with and against thyself
[Bifold] authority, where reason can revolt
Without perdition, and loss assume all reason
Without revolt. This is and is not Cressid.
Within my soul there doth conduce a fight   155
Of this strange nature, that a thing inseparate
Divides more wider than the sky and earth,
And yet the spacious breadth of this division
Admits no orifex for a point as subtle
As Ariachne's broken woof to enter.   160

---

139 critics cynical cavillers. **140 depravation** defamation, disparagement. **square** measure. **general sex** female sex in general. **141 rule** ruler, yardstick. **144 on's** on his, of his. **147 sanctimony** a holy thing. **150 discourse** reasoning. **151–4 That cause . . . Without revolt** N. **151 cause** reasoning. **152 Bifold** F *By foule.* **155 doth conduce** goes on. **156 inseparate** single, whole, unified. **159 orifex** orifice, opening. **160 Ariachne's broken woof** a spider web N.

Instance, O instance, strong as Pluto's gates!
Cressid is mine, tied with the bonds of heaven.
Instance, O instance, strong as heaven itself!
The bonds of heaven are slipp'd, dissolv'd, and
  loos'd,
And with another knot, five finger tied,   165
The fractions of her faith, orts of her love,
The fragments, scraps, the bits, and greasy relics
Of her ore-eaten faith are bound to Diomed.
  Ulysses. May worthy Troilus be half attached
With that which here his passion doth express?   170
  Troilus. Ay, Greek, and that shall be divulged well
In characters as red as Mars his heart,
Inflam'd with Venus. Never did young man fancy
With so eternal and so fix'd a soul.
Hark, Greek. As much [as] I do Cressid love,   175
So much by weight hate I her Diomed.
That sleeve is mine that he'll bear in his helm.
Were it a casque compos'd by Vulcan's skill,
My sword should bite it. Not the dreadful spout
Which shipmen do the hurricano call,   180
Constring'd in mass by the almighty [sun],
Shall dizzy with more clamor Neptune's ear
In his descent than shall my prompted sword,
Falling on Diomed.
  Thersites. He'll tickle it for his concupy.   185

---

161 **Instance** example, evidence, proof. 165 **five finger tied** tied
by mere human hands. 166 **orts** leavings, scraps. 168 **ore-eaten**
eaten over, picked over already. 169 **May** can. **attached** seriously
involved in. 172 **characters** letters. 173 **fancy** love. 175 **As much
as** from F2; Q and F *as much.* **Cressid** F *Cressida.* 179 **spout**
waterspout. 181 **Constring'd** brought together. **sun** F *Fenne.* 183
descent depths. **prompted** ready. 185 **concupy** concubine.

Troilus. O Cressid! O false Cressid! False, false, false!
Let all untruths stand by thy stained name
And they'll seem glorious.
   Ulysses.   O, contain yourself.
Your passion draws ears hither.   189

Enter Aeneas.

Aeneas. I have been seeking you this hour, my lord.
Hector by this is arming him in Troy.
Ajax, your guard, stays to conduct you home.
   Troilus. Have with you, prince. My courteous lord, adieu.
Farewell, revolted fair. And Diomed,
Stand fast and wear a castle on thy head.   195
   Ulysses. I'll bring you to the gates.
   Troilus.   Accept distracted thanks.
         Exeunt Troilus, Aeneas, and Ulysses.
Thersites. Would I could meet that rogue, Diomed.
I would croak like a raven; I would bode, I would
bode. Patroclus will give me anything for the intelli-
gence of this whore. The parrot will not do more
for an almond than he for a commodious drab.
Lechery, lechery, still wars and lechery! Nothing
else holds fashion. A burning divel take them!
                           [Exit.]

192 stays waits. 200–1 parrot . . . almond N. 201 **commodious**
accommodating. 202 **still** always. SD **Exit**: Not in F.

SCENE 3

Enter Hector and Andromache.

Andromache. When was my lord so much urgently
  temper'd
To stop his ears against admonishment?
Unarm, unarm, and do not fight today.
  Hector. You train me to offend you. Get you gone.
By the everlasting gods, I'll go!   5
  Andromache. My dreams will sure prove ominous to
  the day.
  Hector. No more, I say.

Enter Cassandra.

Cassandra.   Where is my brother Hector?
  Andromache. Here, sister, arm'd and bloody in
  intent.
Consort with me in loud and dear petition,
Pursue we him on knees; for I have dreamt   10
Of bloody turbulence, and this whole night
Hath nothing been but shapes and forms of slaugh-
  ter.
  Cassandra. O, 'tis true!
  Hector.   Ho! Bid my trumpet sound.
  Cassandra. No notes of sally, for the heavens, sweet
  brother.
  Hector. Be gone, I say! The gods have heard me
  swear.   15
  Cassandra. The gods are deaf to hot and peevish
  vows;

1 **temper'd** disposed. 4 **train** invite, lure. 9 **dear** honorable. 16
peevish silly, foolish.

125

They are polluted off'rings, more abhorr'd
Than spotted livers in the sacrifice.

Andromache. O, be persuaded. Do not count it holy
To hurt by being just. It is as lawful,   20
For we would give much, to use violent thefts
And rob in behalf of charity.

Cassandra. It is the purpose that makes strong the
   vow,
But vows to every purpose must not hold.
Unarm, sweet Hector.

Hector.   Hold you still, I say!   25
Mine honor keeps the weather of my fate.
Life every man holds dear, but the dear man
Holds honor far more precious-dear than life.

Enter Troilus.

How now, young man? Meanst thou to fight today?
Andromache. Cassandra, call my father to per-
   suade.   *Exit Cassandra.*
Hector. No, faith, young Troilus. Doff thy har-
   ness, youth.   31
I am today i' th' vein of chivalry.
Let grow thy sinews till their knots be strong,
And tempt not yet the brushes of the war.
Unarm thee, go. And doubt thou not, brave boy,
I'll stand today for thee and me and Troy.   36

Troilus. Brother, you have a vice of mercy in you
Which better fits a lion than a man.

Hector. What vice is that? Good Troilus, chide
   me for it.

21 For . . . much because we would like to give much N.
26 keeps the weather of has superiority over, has the wind of.
27 dear man honorable or noble man N. 31 harness armor. 34
brushes attacks, clashes. 38 lion N.

Troilus. When many times the captive Grecian falls,
Even in the fan and wind of your fair sword,   41
You bid them rise and live.
Hector.   O, 'tis fair play.
Troilus. Fool's play, by heaven, Hector!
Hector.   How now, how now?
Troilus. For th' love of all the gods,
Let's leave the hermit Pity with our mothers;   45
And when we have our armors buckled on,
The venom'd vengeance ride upon our swords,
Spur them to ruthful work, rein them from ruth.
Hector. Fie, savage, fie!
Troilus.   Hector, then 'tis wars.
Hector. Troilus, I would not have you fight today.
Troilus. Who should withhold me?   51
Not fate, obedience, nor the hand of Mars
Beck'ning with fiery truncheon my retire;
Not Priamus and Hecuba on knees,
Their eyes oregalled with recourse of tears,   55
Nor you my brother with your true sword drawn
Oppos'd to hinder me, should stop my way
But by my ruin.

Enter Priam and Cassandra.

Cassandra. Lay hold upon him, Priam; hold him
          fast.
He is thy crutch. Now if thou lose thy stay,   60
Thou on him leaning and all Troy on thee,
Fall all together.
Priam.   Come, Hector come. Go back.
Thy wife hath dreamt, thy mother hath had visions,

41 **fan** air current. 48 **ruthful** pitiful, i.e. violent and tragic.
53 **truncheon** staff or baton, sometimes used as signal to stop
fighting.

Cassandra doth foresee, and I myself
Am like a prophet suddenly enrapt   65
To tell thee that this day is ominous.
Therefore, come back.

Hector.   Aeneas is afield,
And I do stand engag'd to many Greeks,
Even in the faith of valor, to appear   69
This morning to them.

Priam.   Ay, but thou shalt not go.

Hector. I must not break my faith.
You know me dutiful; therefore dear sir,
Let me not shame respect, but give me leave
To take that course by your consent and voice
Which you do here forbid me, royal Priam.   75

Cassandra. O Priam, yield not to him.

Andromache.   Do not, dear father.

Hector. Andromache, I am offended with you.
Upon the love you bear me, get you in.   78

                         Exit Andromache.

Troilus. This foolish, dreaming, superstitious girl
Makes all these bodements.

Cassandra.   O farewell, dear Hector.
Look how thou diest! Look how thy eye turns pale!
Look how thy wounds [do] bleed at many vents!
Hark how Troy roars, how Hecuba cries out,
How poor Andromache shrills her dolor forth!
Behold distraction, frenzy, and amazement,   85
Like witless antics one another meet,
And all cry, 'Hector! Hector's dead! O Hector!'

Troilus. Away, away.

---

69 **faith of valor** promises involving a soldier's honor. 73 **shame
respect** disgrace the respect I owe you. 80 **bodements** forebodings.
82 **do** F *doth.* 86 **antics** madmen.

Cassandra. Farewell. Yes, soft! Hector, I take my
    leave.   89
Thou dost thyself and all our Troy deceive.   *Exit.*
Hector. You are amaz'd, my liege, at her exclaim.
Go in and cheer the town; we'll forth and fight,
Do deeds of praise and tell you them at night.
Priam. Farewell. The gods with safety stand about
    thee.   94
    [*Exeunt Priam and Hector severally.*] *Alarum.*
Troilus. They are at it, hark! Proud Diomed, be-
    lieve
I come to lose my arm or win my sleeve.

Enter Pandar.

Pandarus. Do you hear, my lord? Do you hear?
Troilus. What now?
Pandarus. Here's a letter come from yond poor
girl.   100
Troilus. Let me read.
Pandarus. A whoreson tisick, a whoreson rascally
tisick so troubles me, and the foolish fortune of this
girl, and what one thing, what another, that I shall
leave you one o' th's days. And I have a rheum in
mine eyes too, and such an ache in my bones, that
unless a man were curst, I cannot tell what to think
on't. What says she there?   108
  Troilus. Words, words, mere words, no matter
    from the heart;
Th' effect doth operate another way.
                    [*He tears the letter.*]
Go, wind, to wind! There turn and change together.
My love with words and errors still she feeds,

91 **exclaim** exclamations. 102 **tisick** lung congestion, cough. 110
effect real meaning.

But edifies another with her deeds.

Pandarus. Why, but hear you?   114

Troilus. Hence, brother lacky! Ignomy and shame
Pursue thy life and live aye with thy name!

Exeunt.

SCENE 4

Alarum. Enter Thersites in excursion.

Thersites. Now they are clapper-clawing one another, I'll go look on. That dissembling abominable
varlet, Diomed, has got that same scurvy, doting,
foolish young knave's sleeve of Troy there in his
helm. I would fain see them meet, that that same
young Troyan ass that loves the whore there might
send that Greekish whoremasterly villain with the
sleeve back to the dissembling, luxurious drab of a
sleeveless errant. O' th' tother side, the policy of
those crafty swearing rascals—that [stale] old-
mouse-eaten dry cheese, Nestor, and that same dog-
fox Ulysses—is not prov'd worth a blackberry. They
set me up, in policy, that mongrel cur Ajax against
that dog of as bad a kind, Achilles. And now is the
cur Ajax prouder than the cur Achilles and will not
arm today. Whereupon, the Grecians began to proclaim barbarism, and policy grows into an ill opinion.   18

114–16 Why . . . name N. 115 Ignomy ignominy. SD in excursion running onstage. 8 luxurious lecherous. 8–9 of a sleeveless
errant on a useless errand. 10 stale F *stole.* 13 set me up set up.
13 in policy craftily. 16–17 proclaim barbarism follow anarchic
barbarity rather than ordered policy.

Enter Diomed and Troilus.

Soft! Here comes sleeve and th' other.

Troilus. Fly not; for shouldst thou take the River
    Styx   20
I would swim after.

Diomedes.   Thou dost miscall retire.
I do not fly, but advantageous care
Withdrew me from the odds of multitude.
Have at thee!   24

Thersites. Hold thy whore, Grecian! Now, for thy
whore, Troyan! Now the sleeve, now the sleeve!

                [Exeunt Diomed and Troilus.]

Enter Hector.

Hector. What are thou, Greek? Art thou for Hec-
    tor's match?
Art thou of blood and honor?

Thersites. No, no! I am a rascal, a scurvy railing
knave, a very filthy rogue.   30

Hector. I do believe thee. Live.   *[Exit.]*

Thersites. God a mercy that thou wilt believe me;
but a plague break thy neck for frighting me. What's
become of the wenching rogues? I think they have
swallowed one another. I would laugh at that miracle;
yet in a sort, lechery eats itself. I'll seek them.   *Exit.*

22 **advantageous care** care for my own advantage. 27 **Hector's
match** N.

SCENE 5

Enter Diomed and Servants.

Diomedes. Go, go, my servant, take thou Troilus'
    horse.
Present the fair steed to my Lady Cressid.
Fellow, commend my service to her beauty;
Tell her I have chastis'd the amorous Troyan   4
And am her knight by proof.
    Servant.   I go, my lord.   [*Exit.*]

Enter Agamemnon.

Agamemnon. Renew, renew! The fierce Polidamus
Hath beat down Menon; bastard Margarelon
Hath Doreus prisoner
And stands colossus-wise waving his beam
Upon the pashed corses of the kings   10
Epistropus and Cedus. Polixenes is slain;
Amphimacus and Thous deadly hurt;
Patroclus tane or slain, and Palamedes
Sore hurt and bruis'd. The dreadful Sagittary
Appalls our numbers. Haste we, Diomed,   15
To reinforcement, or we perish all.

Enter Nestor.

Nestor. Go bear Patroclus' body to Achilles,
And bid the snail-pac'd Ajax arm for shame.
There is a thousand Hectors in the field.
Now here he fights on Galathe, his horse,   20
And there lacks work; anon he's there afoot,

6–13 Polidamus . . . Palamedes N. 9 beam lance. 10 pashed
smashed, mangled. corses corpses. 13 tane taken. 14 Sagittary N.
    132

And there they fly or die, like scaled sculls
Before the belching whale; then is he yonder,
And there the straying Greeks, ripe for his edge,
Fall down before him like the mower's swath.   25
Here, there, and everywhere he leaves and takes,
Dexterity so obeying appetite
That what he will he does, and does so much
That proof is call'd impossibility.

Enter Ulysses.

Ulysses. O courage, courage, princes! Great Achilles   30
Is arming, weeping, cursing, vowing vengeance.
Patroclus' wounds have rous'd his drowsy blood,
Together with his mangled Myrmidons
That noseless, handless, hack'd, and chipp'd come to
    him,
Crying on Hector. Ajax hath lost a friend   35
And foams at mouth, and he is arm'd and at it,
Roaring for Troilus, who hath done today
Mad and fantastic execution,
Engaging and redeeming of himself
With such a careless force and forceless care   40
As if that luck, in very spite of cunning,
Bade him win all.

Enter Ajax.

Ajax. Troilus! Thou coward, Troilus!   *Exit.*
Diomedes.   Ay, there, there!
Nestor. So, so, we draw together.   *Exit.*

22 **scaled sculls** schools of fish. 25 **swath** grain cut by scythe.
29 **proof** accomplished fact. 35 **Crying on** exclaiming about. 38
execution five syllables here.

Enter Achilles.

Achilles. Where is this Hector?
Come, come, thou boy-queller, shew thy face! 45
Know what it is to meet Achilles angry.
Hector, where's Hector? I will none but Hector.

[*Exeunt.*]

SCENE 6

Enter Ajax.

Ajax. Troilus, thou coward Troilus, shew thy
head!

Enter Diomed.

Diomedes. Troilus, I say! Where's Troilus?
Ajax. What wouldst thou?
Diomedes. I would correct him.
Ajax. Were I the general, thou shouldst have my
office 4
Ere that correction. Troilus, I say! What, Troilus!

Enter Troilus.

Troilus. O traitor Diomed!
Turn thy false face, thou traitor,
And pay thy life thou ow'st me for my horse!
Diomedes. Ha, art thou there? 9
Ajax. I'll fight with him alone. Stand, Diomed.
Diomedes. He is my prize. I will not look upon.

45 **queller** killer. SD **Exeunt** N. 5 **Ere that correction** N. 11 **look upon** be a spectator.

Troilus. Come, both you cogging Greeks. Have at
   you both!

            Exeunt Troilus [, *Ajax, and Diomed*].

Enter Hector.

Hector. Yea, Troilus? O well fought, my youngest
   brother!

Enter Achilles.

Achilles. Now do I see thee. Have at thee Hector!
Hector. Pause, if thou wilt.   15
Achilles. I do disdain thy courtesy, proud Troyan.
Be happy that my arms are out of use;
My rest and negligence befriends thee now,
But thou anon shalt hear of me again;   19
Till when, go seek thy fortune.   *Exit.*
Hector.   Fare thee well.
I would have been much more a fresher man
Had I expected thee. How now, my brother?

Enter Troilus.

Troilus. Ajax hath tane Aeneas! Shall it be?
No, by the flame of yonder glorious heaven,
He shall not carry him. I'll be tane too,   25
Or bring him off. Fate hear me what I say;
I reck not though thou end my life today.   *Exit.*

Enter One in armor.

Hector. Stand, stand, thou Greek! Thou art a
   goodly mark.
No? Wilt thou not? I like thy armor well;

12 **cogging** defrauding. SD **Exeunt . . . Diomed** F has merely
Exit Troilus. 18 **rest and negligence** i.e. his long inactivity has
made him rusty. 25 **carry** prevail, have victory over.

I'll frush it and unlock the rivets all,   30
But I'll be master of it. Wilt thou not, beast, abide?
Why then, fly on. I'll hunt thee for thy hide.

                            [*Exeunt.*]

SCENE 7

Enter Achilles with Myrmidons.

Achilles. Come here about me, you my Myrmidons.
Mark what I say: Attend me where I wheel,
Strike not a stroke, but keep yourselves in breath;
And when I have the bloody Hector found,
Empale him with your weapons round about.   5
In fellest manner execute your arms.
Follow me, sirs, and my proceeding eye.
It is decreed Hector the great must die.

                      Exit [*with followers*].

Enter Thersites, Menelaus, and Paris.

Thersites. The cuckold and the cuckold maker are
at it. Now bull! Now dog! Low, Paris, low! Now my
double hen'd sparrow! Low, Paris, low! The bull has
the game. 'Ware horns, ho!   12

                    Exit Paris and Menelaus.

Enter Bastard.

Bastard. Turn, slave, and fight!
Thersites. What art thou?
Bastard. A bastard son of Priam's.   15

30 frush smash. SD **Exeunt** F *Exit.* 2 **wheel** turn, go. 5 **Empale**
'surround,' as with a fence. 6 **execute** employ, make use of.
arms F *arme.* 10 **Low** sound of a bull (a horned beast). 11 **double
hen'd sparrow** N.

Thersites. I am a bastard too. I love bastards. I am a bastard begot, bastard instructed, bastard in mind, bastard in valor, in everything illegitimate. One bear will not bite another, and wherefore should one bastard? Take heed; the quarrel's most ominous to us; if the son of a whore fight for a whore, he tempts judgment. Farewell, bastard.   22

Bastard. The divel take thee, coward.   *Exeunt.*

SCENE 8

Enter Hector

Hector. Most putrified core, so fair without,
Thy goodly armor thus hath cost thy life.
Now is my day's work done. I'll take good breath.
Rest, sword; thou hast thy fill of blood and death.

Enter Achilles and his Myrmidons.

Achilles. Look, Hector, how the sun begins to set;
How ugly night comes breathing at his heels,   6
Even with the vail and darking of the sun.
To close the day up, Hector's life is done.

Hector. I am unarm'd. Forgo this vantage, Greek.

Achilles. Strike, fellows, strike! This is the man I
     seek.   10
So Ilion, fall thou; now Troy sink down!
Here lies thy heart, thy sinews, and thy bone.
On Myrmidons! Cry you all amain:
'Achilles hath the mighty Hector slain.'   *Retreat.*
Hark, a retreat upon our Grecian part.   15

---

1 **putrified** four syllables here. 3 **breath** breathing space, rest.
7 **vail** setting.

Greek. The Troyan trumpets sound the like, my
    lord.

Achilles. The dragon wing of night orespreads the
    earth

And, sticklerlike, the armies separates.

My half-supp'd sword that frankly would have fed,

Pleas'd with this dainty bait, thus goes to bed.   20

Come, tie his body to my horse's tail;

Along the field I will the Troyan trail.   *Exeunt.*

SCENE 9

Sound retreat. Shout.

*Enter Agamemnon, Ajax, Menelaus, Nestor,
Diomed, and the rest, marching.*

Agamemnon. Hark, hark! What shout is that?

Nestor.   Peace, drums.

Soldier. [*Within.*] Achilles! Achilles! Hector's
    slain! Achilles!

Diomedes. The bruit is, Hector's slain and by
    Achilles.

Ajax. If it be so, yet bragless let it be.

Great Hector was a man as good as he.   5

Agamemnon. March patiently along. Let one be
    sent

To pray Achilles see us at our tent.

If in his death the gods have us befriended,

Great Troy is ours, and our sharp wars are ended.
    Exeunt.

16 **Greek** one of the Myrmidons. **sound** F *sounds.* 18 **stickler—**
an arbiter at a duel. 19 **frankly** abundantly, freely. 2 **Within Q**
only. 3 **bruit** clamor, rumor.

138

SCENE 10

Enter Aeneas, Paris, Antenor, and Deiphobus.

Aeneas. Stand, ho! Yet are we masters of the field.
Never go home. Here starve we out the night.

Enter Troilus.

Troilus. Hector is slain.
All.   Hector? The gods forbid!
Troilus. He's dead; and at the murtherer's horse's
    tail,   4
In beastly sort dragg'd through the shameful field.
Frown on, you heavens; effect your rage with speed!
Sit, gods, upon your thrones, and smile at Troy!
I say, at once let your brief plagues be mercy,
And linger not our sure destructions on.   9
  Aeneas. My lord, you do discomfort all the host.
  Troilus. You understand me not that tell me so.
I do not speak of flight, of fear, of death,
But dare all imminence that gods and men
Address their dangers in. Hector is gone.
Who shall tell Priam so? Or Hecuba?   15
Let him that will a screechowl aye be call'd
Go in to Troy, and say there, 'Hector's dead.'
There is a word will Priam turn to stone,
Make wells and Niobes of the maids and wives,
Cool statues of the youth, and in a word,   20
Scare Troy out of itself. But march away;
Hector is dead. There is no more to say.
Stay yet. You vile abominable tents,

7 smile N. 13 imminence impending evil. 14 Address prepare.
139

Thus proudly pight upon our Phrygian plains,
Let Titan rise as early as he dare,   25
I'll through and through you! And thou great-siz'd
    coward,
No space of earth shall sunder our two hates.
I'll haunt thee like a wicked conscience still,
That moldeth goblins swift as frenzy's thoughts.
Strike a free march to Troy. With comfort go.   30
Hope of revenge shall hide our inward woe.

Enter Pandarus.

Pandarus. But hear you? Hear you?
Troilus. Hence, broker-lacky! Ignomy and shame
Pursue thy life and live aye with thy name.   34
              Exeunt [all but Pandarus].
Pandarus. A goodly med'cine for mine aching
bones. O world, world, world! Thus is the poor
agent despis'd. O traitors and bawds! How earnestly are you set awork, and how ill requited! Why
should our endeavor be so desir'd, and the performance so loath'd? What verse for it? What
instance for it? Let me see.   41

> *Full merrily the humble bee doth sing*
> *Till he hath lost his honey and his sting;*
> *And being once subdu'd in armed tail,*
> *Sweet honey and sweet notes together fail.*   45

Good traders in the flesh, set this in your painted
cloths.
As many as be here of Pandar's hall,
Your eyes half out, weep out at Pandar's fall;
Or if you cannot weep, yet give some groans,   50

24 **pight** pitched. 25 **Titan** the sun. SD **all but Pandarus.** Q only.
46–7 **painted cloths** wall hangings N.
   140

Though not for me, yet for your aching bones.
Brethren and sisters of the hold-door trade,
Some two months hence my will shall here be made.
It should be now, but that my fear is this:
Some galled goose of Winchester would hiss.   55
Till then, I'll sweat and seek about for eases,
And at that time bequeath you my diseases.

[Exit.]

FINIS

52 **hold-door** pimp, pander (those who hold the door to ensure privacy). 55 **galled goose of Winchester** N. 56 **sweat** N. SD **Exit** F *Exeunt.*

NOTES

The Prologue

17 Antenonidus The spelling of this name differs from the form we find in earlier writers who name the gates; but since there is no real agreement even among these earlier authorities, the F reading has been allowed to stand.

19 Sperr up This is an emendation introduced in Theobald's edition for the unsatisfactory reading in F.

23–5 prologue arm'd . . . argument The prologue comes not to boast of the excellence of the author or the actors, and he is dressed in armor simply because it is appropriate to the warlike argument of the play. Some scholars have interpreted this passage as a reference to Jonson's satirical play, *The Poetaster*, and have further interpreted the whole play of *Troilus and Cressida* as Shakespeare's rejoinder to Jonson.

Act I, Scene 1

24–5 here's . . . hereafter There's yet more hereafter in the word *tarry*, i.e. *the kneading*, etc.

30 So . . . thence Troilus calls himself a traitor for admitting that Cressida is ever out of his thoughts. Then he goes on to say that whenever she goes from them, she immediately comes back.

43 And *And* in this meaning appears frequently throughout any Renaissance play, and in modern editions it is usually spelled *an*. In this play and in F it is almost always spelled *and*.

60 spirit of sense This phrase has been much discussed, and there is no explanation which is generally agreed upon. Perhaps Shakespeare means the essential, invisible spirit of sensation. In a series of soft things being compared with the softness of Cressida's hand, this intangible, immaterial item is certainly not out of place.

79 fair . . . Sunday Cressida would be as beautiful in her poorest clothes as Helen in her finest.

84 father Cressida's father was Calchas, a priest, who had deserted the Trojan cause to go over to the Greeks. Shakespeare, in treating Calchas later on in Act III, makes no reference to the legend that he had been told to do so by Apollo.

105 Ilium In this play, as in the medieval authorities for the Troilus story, Ilium always means specifically the palace of Priam rather than the entire city of Troy.

115 horn The horn joke was omnipresent in the Elizabethan period. A man whose wife was unfaithful to him was pictured as having invisible cuckold's horns on his head. The joke appears throughout this play, almost as often as Menelaus is mentioned.

122 togither This spelling of 'together' is not infrequent in Shakespeare's plays; for the rhyme *thither : togither* see Helge Kökeritz, *Shakespeare's Pronunciation* (New Haven, Yale University Press, 1953), p. 187.

Act I, Scene 2

13 nephew Actually Ajax was Hector's cousin. Much earlier Priam's sister, Hesione, had been carried off to Greece and there, according to one legend, was married to Telamon and bore Ajax. Thus Ajax was Priam's nephew and Hector's cousin. This relationship is mentioned again in II.2 and IV.5.

22 humors In Renaissance medicine the four humors (blood, yellow bile, black bile, and phlegm) were fluids secreted by various organs of the body. These fluids were thought to determine not only physical health but temperament, personality, and behavior. When the secretions were functioning properly and the right proportions of each were maintained, health resulted; but if one humor became excessive, certain aberrations were likely to appear. The word also had an extended, less technical usage, meaning 'caprice' or 'mood.'

23–4 valor . . . discretion His valor is crushed into or mixed thoroughly with folly, and his folly is further mixed or sauced with discretion.

43 cousin This word was very loosely applied in Elizabethan English to virtually any collateral relationship. Actually, Cressida was Pandarus' niece.

76 Condition By the impossible nature of the condition, we gather that Pandarus is contradicting Cressida.

78 a This unaccented form of 'he' was probably a neutral [ə] sound, though the spelling is uniformly *a* in the Renaissance texts. It will be hereafter printed without gloss or comment.

79–80 time . . . end This was a proverbial phrase, meaning something like 'Time will tell.'

88 will Some modern editors emend this word to *wit*. Both F and Q have *will*, however, and if we take it to refer to Troilus' will power or strength of will no emendation is necessary.

118 tapster's arithmetic The tapsters or drawers of beer in the alehouses were proverbially poor at adding.

203 nod The related word, 'noddy,' a simpleton, forms the punning basis for Cressida's next speech. 'He who is already rich in foolishness (a noddy) shall receive more if Troilus give him a nod.'

208 brave Here and elsewhere in the play this word probably has double or triple connotations, since the meaning could be 'courageous,' or simply 'splendid,' 'fine,' or sometimes 'showy,' 'gaudy.'

266 date's out The pun here depends on the meaning of *date* with reference to time: 'the man's time is up' or 'he's out of date.'

271 mask Renaissance women often wore masks to protect their complexions from the elements.

275 watch Puns on the various meanings of *watch* and *ward* run throughout this passage. Cressida means here that she will prevent his telling by keeping watch on him.

288 To bring This is a rare Elizabethan slang idiom, possibly meaning 'with a vengeance.'

302 Achievement . . . beseech This cryptic epigram is evidently not proverbial but rather original with Cressida. It probably means that men use entreaty when the lady is ungained, but change to peremptory language when the object is achieved.

Act I, Scene 3

8 diverts Both F and Q read thus, although modern usage demands *divert*. Such plurals formed with -*s* by analogy with the singular were common in Shakespeare's day and constituted an acceptable variant to the form without -*s*.

15 Bias The bowling balls of the time were not true spheres but had a bias or added weight on one side. Often in Shakespeare this word is extended metaphorically to other matters, as it is here.

23 Fortune's The concept of the goddess Fortune was a favorite idea which the Elizabethans inherited from the Middle Ages. She might befriend a person without reason and bring him success, or just as capriciously plunge him into misery.

54 Retorts F reads *Retyres*. Various emendations have been suggested for this meaningless reading. The word *Retorts* was first proposed by Dyce (ed. 1857) and has been accepted by most modern editors, although there is no way of knowing exactly what Shakespeare wrote.

60 To Agamemnon There is no indication of the person addressed in the early texts, but this and the following line make sense only if addressed to Agamemnon and Nestor respectively.

65 hatch'd The phrase *hatch'd in silver* probably refers to Nestor's white hair.

73 masty The rare word *Masticke* in the Folio (this passage does not occur in Q) has occasioned many ingenious explanations. Professor Kökeritz suggests very plausibly that the printer misread *mastie* (mastif) as *mastic*, which he set up in type with a conventional *ck* and a mute *e*.

85 center Shakespeare is here using the Ptolemaic concept of the cosmos.

89 Sol The sun was considered a planet in Ptolemaic astronomy.

92 aspects According to the lore of astrology, certain relative positions or aspects of planets are supposed to have harmful effects on earthly activities.

118 her This *her* may be a mere mistake in F for *their*, which is the Q reading. It is perfectly possible, however, that this is the old form for the third person genitive plural (Chaucer's *here*), common in southern texts up to the beginning of the 16th century, although archaic by Shakespeare's time.

128–9 purpose . . . climb The purpose of those who neglect degree is to climb the social ladder to the next step above. This process goes downward, or *backward*, pace by pace through the ranks as specified in the succeeding lines.

145

157 **orewrested** Shakespeare is drawing a metaphor from stringed musical instruments. The wrest was the pin used for tightening the string.

168 **Vulcan and his wife** The god Vulcan was always pictured as particularly ugly, while Venus was, of course, extremely beautiful.

212 **Thetis' sons** Achilles was Thetis' son. Nestor means that if it be granted that physical force is superior to mental powers, then anyone mounted on Achilles' horse would be as great as Achilles.

238–9 **Jove's . . . heart** When Jove approves, nothing is so full of courage (as a Trojan).

339–41 **For . . . general** The outcome of the combat, although it actually applies to only two particular persons, shall decide the amount of praise or shame attributed to the Greeks and Trojans in general.

342–5 **And in . . . large** The figure here refers to the table of contents of a book. From the brief indication of the 'index' one sees in reduced form the contents of the whole volume.

353–5 **Which . . . the limbs** Deighton (ed. 1906) paraphrases this passage thus: 'And if this belief (i.e. of the Trojans, that they will be victorious) is entertained it will energise the limbs of those who hold it, just as those limbs energise the swords and bows they wield.'

Act II, Scene 1

14 **whinid'st** Since this word appears nowhere else, it has produced many ingenious emendations. Many editors have avoided it by substituting the Q reading, *unsalted*, but this is also unsatisfactory because salt is not normally required for leavening. The most plausible suggestion has been that of Upton (*Critical Observations*, 1746), who noted that *whinid'st* could be a dialectal pronunciation of 'vinewedest' or 'vinidest' (finewedest), meaning 'most mouldy.' This view is supported by Kökeritz, *Shakespeare's Pronunciation*, p. 323.

33 **Cerberus . . . Proserpina's** Cerberus was the three-headed

dog who guarded the Greek Hades. Proserpina was the beautiful wife of Pluto, the god of the underworld.

54 Mars his idiot This construction, called the *his*-genitive, was originally due to a grammatical misconception. The genitive ending *-es* in a word like 'Marses' was sometimes thought to be a separate element, i.e. 'Mars is,' and this 'is' was thought to be equivalent to *his*. It was used very commonly throughout the Renaissance and even later. It appears frequently later on in this play.

112 To Achilles! to Ajax! This is uttered as if a call urging on a team of oxen.

119 brooch Many modern editors emend this word to *brach*. Since it appears as *brooch*, however, in Q and all the Folios, it is likely that the word is correct as it stands. It would not be surprising if Thersites were making a highly obscene accusation, for *brooch* or 'broach' in the 16th century meant, among other things, a 'pointed rod, spit or pricker.' (cf. OED).

Act II, Scene 2

19 tithe This word also meant anything paid by way of offering or sacrifice. The ambiguity adds meaning to this passage.

45 And fly . . . Jove F has this line misplaced two lines further along. The Q placement is obviously preferable.

58–60 And the . . . merit This passage might be paraphrased: 'That will is foolish which inclines to something which it unwholesomely likes without taking into account some idea of the absolute merit of the thing liked.'

166 Aristotle In the *Nicomachean Ethics*, Aristotle indicated that political philosophy was unsuitable for young men. The term *moral* in the 16th century embraced the realm of political ethics as well as other things.

172 adders It was a popular belief in Shakespeare's time that adders were deaf, or could stop up their ears at will.

Act II, Scene 3

25–6 gilt counterfeit . . . slipp'd Thersites is punning on the meaning of 'slip' as a counterfeit coin.

147

41 cheese The practice of eating cheese after a meal was supposed to aid digestion. Also a noble lord often called in his fool to entertain him after a meal. Achilles thus combines the two in a facetious metaphor.

81 shent Neither the Q nor F reading makes sense in this passage, and most modern editors accept the emendation *shent* of Theobald.

96–9 matter . . . Achilles Nestor and Ulysses are playing with the word *argument*. Nestor says that Ajax will lack subject matter for this railing if he has lost Thersites. Ulysses replies that he has a new *argument* for railing, namely Achilles, who took away Thersites.

101 counsel Q has *composure*, which makes sense in this passage, but not very different sense from the F reading.

103 knits not, The punctuation here is from the Q. F has *knits, not folly* etc., which contains the obverse of the same idea.

109 flexure Although the F reading makes sense of a sort, the Q word is preferable, since this whole passage controverts an old notion, still current in Shakespeare's day, that elephants have no joints. It adds an idea from a proverb that elephants, like great men, are too proud to bow, or 'make a leg.'

128–32 And worthier . . . predominance A worthier man than he here attends his rude aloofness, foregoes the deference due to the holy strength of his position (commander-in-chief), and submits in a passive way to his capricious superiority.

178 Kingdom'd Achilles is metaphorically considered a kingdom containing warring factions.

199 coals to Cancer Cancer is the sign of the zodiac which the sun enters at the summer solstice. Thus this line means 'and add more heat to summer.'

215 let his humor's blood In the word *humor's* the apostrophe undoubtedly means that it is a contracted form of *humorous*, which is the reading of Q. *Humorous* means here both 'full of humors' and 'capricious.'

220 eat swords This may be a printer's error for *eat's words*, i.e. *eat his words*. However, there are other scornful references in Shakespeare to eating swords (*Much Ado about Nothing*, IV.1.273; *Anthony and Cleopatra*, III.13.199–200).

223 **shares** This line is sometimes taken as a topical allusion to the financial arrangements of Shakespeare's company. When the Globe theater was built in 1599, its ownership was divided into ten shares. Thus Ulysses would seem to mean that Ajax would have all (pride), not just half.

225 **He's . . . warm** Both F and Q give this sentence to Ajax' preceding speech. It makes more sense, however, as part of Nestor's speech, and most modern editors print it so. None of the asides in this scene are so marked in F, but it is clear there are several speeches Ajax is not meant to hear.

228 **My lord** Although the F does not indicate it with a scene direction, Ulysses quite obviously shifts his address to Agamemnon at this point.

250 **Milo** Milo was a semilegendary athlete of Greece who bore a four-year-old bull forty yards, killed it with one blow, and ate it.

Act III, Scene 1

13 **honor** The servant is punning on the word *honor*, as he does in the next speech on the word *grace*. Pandarus does not catch the joke.

34 **love's invisible soul** Helen, as a very symbol of love and beauty, a mortal Venus, is here hyperbolically considered the very essence or spirit of love.

40-1 **complimental assault** Pandarus in this speech and in his next is using rather affectedly courtly language. *Complimental* refers to paying his compliments or respects in a formal way.

42 **Sodden** This is the old past participle of 'seethe.' The servant twists Pandarus' word by applying another meaning common at the time. Hot steaming baths were used as a remedy for venereal disease, and a person in them was in a sense *sodden*. This naturally suggests the 'stews' or brothels of his next pun.

SD **Helena** This older form of the name Helen is used nowhere else in the play.

44 **Fair** Throughout this speech Pandarus is employing a rather exaggerated rhetorical trick with his frequent repetition of the word fair as an adjective, adverb, and noun, sometimes meaning 'good,' 'fine,' sometimes 'beautiful.'

149

58 fits Paris' remark is not entirely clear; perhaps he means Pandarus deprecates his singing only now and then, by *fits*. A pun is possible, for *fits* also meant the stanzas or sections of a song.

88 Helen Helen's speech here is sometimes made part of Pandarus' preceding speech, and it perhaps fits better there; but since neither F nor Q give any authority for such a shift, and since it is understandable, with a slightly different sense, in Helen's mouth, the F reading has been retained.

115 Love The tenor of this song is highly bawdy, since the pun on *die*, 'experience orgasm' and 'expire,' runs throughout. *Hey ho*, at the end, may be not part of the song but a sigh of Pandarus after finishing.

131 doves Doves were, of course, sacred to Venus, and Paris indicates that eating them has an aphrodisiac effect.

137 vipers Pandarus is jokingly bringing the idea around to the familiar phrase 'generation of vipers' from the Bible (Matt. 3:7), where, of course, it is used in a completely different context.

163 Sweet . . . thee This sentence is part of Helen's preceding speech in F, but is given to the uxorious Paris in Q.

Act III, Scene 2

9–10 Stygian . . . Charon Charon was the boatman who ferried souls across the river Styx to the Greek underworld. The fields of lilies in the next line are the Elysian fields.

43 watch'd Hawks were often tamed by wearing them down through lack of sleep.

50 in fee-farm A *fee-farm* was a grant of land in fee for an indefinite period of time.

52–3 falcon . . . tercel The *falcon* is the female bird and the *tercel* the male. Pandarus is also using a phrase from betting jargon, saying that he would back Cressida against Troilus for any amount.

97–8 envy . . . his truth The worst thing malice can say of him will be to mock him for his fidelity and truth.

133 Coming Many editors emend this word to *Cunning*, but this F and Q reading *Coming* makes excellent sense.

177 plantage In some quarters the belief persists to the present that the growth of vegetation is influenced by the moon.

SD **Exeunt** Troilus and Cressida start off stage after l. 209, and Pandarus stays behind a moment to deliver his leering couplet to the audience.

Act III, Scene 3

4 sight . . . love This passage has been often discussed and emended, and certainly *things to come* would be a more intelligible reading. Both F and Q have *things to love*, however. Possibly Shakespeare meant 'through the insight I have into things which should be loved,' namely life, security, and the winning side. The soothsayer Calchas had previously been informed by the Delphic oracle that Troy would lose the war.

30 pain The phrase *most accepted* may refer to Calchas' acceptance of the hardships, or it may imply that the Greeks have readily accepted his painful services.

134–5 How . . . eyes How some men sneak unnoticed into capricious Fortune's hall, while others, from her point of view, play the fool.

137 feasting Many editors prefer the Q reading, *fasting*, here, but the F makes perfectly good sense and is more directly applicable to Achilles.

162 rear This word is an emendation suggested by Hanmer (ed. 1745). The F has *abject, neere*. Lines 161–2 are missing in Q.

178 give F and Q have *go*. Theobald first used this emendation in his edition of 1733, and it has been accepted by most subsequent editors.

183 sooner The words *begin to* in F were probably drawn down mistakenly from the line above by a copyist or a typesetter.

198 Knows . . . gold 'Knows minutely of the most unsearchable things.' Shakespeare, along with many others in his time, seems to amalgamate the persons of Pluto, god of the lower world, and Plutus, the god of riches.

209 Polixena Daughter of Priam and Hecuba, with whom Achilles had fallen in love. Though not in Homer, this twist in the Troy story was added in later Greek times, and the medieval writers on Troy emphasized it as one of the motives for Achilles' withdrawal from the battle.

216 fool . . . break This line has been variously interpreted. Possibly it means that Achilles should break the thin ice Ajax is sliding over, and thus keep him in his place. Some scholars have taken this as a reference to an actual event which Shakespeare knew about, and have used it as an argument for dating the play.

232 commission . . . blank 'Puts you at the complete mercy of danger.' The metaphor here is drawn from the practice of issuing blank commissions to the collectors of imposts, to be filled in at their discretion.

Act IV, Scene 1

66 which . . . whore? This line has been much discussed. The Q reads *the heavier for a whore*, and neither F nor Q has a question mark. Using the common concept of a whore as a 'light' woman, however, the F reading becomes quite intelligible as a question, and the line supports the idea of equal balance which Diomedes has stated in the previous line.

78 We'll . . . sell This line has caused trouble, mainly because Paris obviously has no intention of selling Helen, except at the very dear price of defeat. It is clear, however, that he is reversing the practice of the chapmen and of Diomedes in favor of silence concerning his commodity.

Act IV, Scene 2

31–2 chipochia This word is probably best explained as an anglicized form of the Italian *cappocchia*, 'simpleton.' Pandarus is here speaking mock baby talk, however, and this may be a mere invented nonce word of endearment.

Act IV, Scene 4

35 rejoindure. This is merely an elaborated spelling of *rejoinder* from *re-* and *joinder* (union) as in *Twelfth Night*, V.1.160.

47 tears After this word in F, but not in Q, there occurs the SD *Enter Aeneas*. This is probably a mistake, for further along at l. 96 Aeneas still speaks *Within*.

49 **genius** In Roman mythology each person was thought to have an attendant spirit or genius which presided over his destiny during life.

56 **When . . . again** Through a typesetter's error this line is given to Troilus in F. Q has it as part of Cressida's speech.

77 **Flowing** This emendation was suggested by Stanton. There is some reason to suspect that there was post-Shakespearean tampering with the text in this passage, either in the theater or the printing shop, for the Q leaves out this word and the entire preceding line. The Q line *And swelling . . . exercise* is a normal pentameter line, and the addition of this word in the F turns it into a hexameter. The F reading has been retained, however, since not only this word but the whole of l. 76 is involved, and it would be hard to prove that that line is not Shakespeare's.

SD **Paris, Aeneas . . .** The F SD reads *Enter the Greeks*, but of course Diomedes is the only Greek who takes part in the ensuing scene.

120 **zeal . . . thee** This is the Q reading, except that the word *seal* of both Q and F was emended to *zeal* by Warburton (ed. 1747). The somewhat garbled F reading for this passage runs: *To shame the seale of my petition towards/ I praising her.*

142 **Let . . . straight** This line is marked *Dio.* in F, and it does not occur in Q. Since it is entirely inappropriate for Diomedes, most editors assume that the *Dio.* was a mistake for *Dei.* and assign the speech to Deiphobus.

Act IV, Scene 5

SD **Calchas** Calchas' name stands thus in the SD of both F and Q, although he does not speak in this scene, and from Diomedes' speech at l. 53 it would seem that he is not present.

29 **And . . . argument** This line was evidently dropped inadvertently by the compositor of F, for the line is needed to explain the action at this point. At the word *thus* Patroclus evidently steps between Menelaus and Cressida and kisses her in his stead.

59 **a coasting** So spelled in both F and Q. It may be that this should be read *accosting*, but it may also be from the verb 'to coast,' to move alongside, as of a ship. In either case the whole

sentence is clearer if *welcome* be taken as the direct object and *a coasting* as the indirect object of *give*.

63 game After this word F, but not Q, has *Exeunt*, but judging from the ensuing scene no one leaves the stage.

83 Ajax . . . blood Ajax, as son of Hesione, Hector's aunt, was closely related to Hector by blood. Cf. I.2.13 N.

96 knight After this word in F, but not in Q, there follow the words, *they call him Troilus*. They evidently are out of place, for they anticipate and duplicate part of l. 108. The later position is preferable, since the identification appears as the culmination of the description.

144 Neoptolymus It is not clear just whom Hector is talking about. Neoptolemus (or Pyrrhus, mentioned above at III.3.210) was Achilles' son, and according to some versions of the Troy legend was eventually responsible for the conclusion of the war, but at this time he had no reputation which could be termed *mirable*. Samuel Johnson suggested that Shakespeare might have taken Neoptolemus to be the family name, and therefore he is here speaking of Achilles.

145 Oyes Both F and Q read (*O yes*), but this was a frequent spelling for the cry 'Oyez,' 'hear ye,' an expression still used in the law courts.

SD Enter . . . rest This stage direction occurs in F but not in Q. It is puzzling since they have probably not left the stage. Perhaps they watched the fight from a distance (possibly from the inner stage) and at this point come forward to the group around the fighters.

198 grandsire Laomedon, father of Priam, years before had been active in some of the incidents leading up to the Trojan War. Nestor's great age at present led the medieval authorities to assume that he also had been an actor in the events of two generations before, although the Greek stories record no fight between Laomedon and Nestor. At I.3.292 Shakespeare has Nestor refer to Laomedon in a slightly different way.

293 doth The F spells this word *dooth*, and it is possible that it did make a perfect rhyme with *tooth*, whatever their common vowel sound. (See *Shakespeare's Pronunciation*, pp. 236 f.)

154

Act V, Scene 1

11 surgeon's box Thersites punningly takes *tent* to mean 'a probe for a wound.'

16 varlot This is the reading of both F and Q and thus it has been retained. There is a temptation to emend the word to *harlot*, as many editors have done, particularly because of Thersites' explanation in l. 18. Perhaps an amalgamation of the word *harlot* and *varlet* was intentional with Thersites. However, *varlots* appears in Q at V.1.93, where no such ambiguity is intended.

21 palsies After this word the Q adds: *raw eyes, dirt-rotten livers, wheezing lungs, bladders full of impostume* (pus), *sciaticas, lime-kilns* (burnings) *i' th' palm, incurable bone-ache, and the riveled fee-simple of the tetter* (absolute ownership of the skin disease). The words *and the like* in F are thought to be a substitution at some later time when the long quarto list of diseases was shortened.

51–3 transformation . . . cuckolds In the Europa story Jupiter transformed himself into a bull. Thus the bull, a horned creature, may be considered, as Thersites puts it, to be *the primitive statue and oblique memorial of cuckolds*, such as Menelaus.

54 shoeing horn. There is probably here another reference to cuckoldry, plus the idea of Menelaus' ineffectual dependence on Agamemnon (hanging on a chain at his leg).

SD Exeunt . . . Ulysses A simple *Exeunt* after l. 87 in Q and F was probably meant as a blanket affair to get the two parties off the stage severally.

91 Brabbler A hound which bayed a great deal but hunted poorly was often called a *brabbler* or a 'babbler.'

Act V, Scene 2

63 potato Potatoes were commonly thought to be aphrodisiac.

89 Nay . . . me This sentence is given to Diomedes in both Q and F. The apparent action of the scene, however, makes it likely that it is part of Cressida's speech.

110–11 likes not me Q has *likes not you*, which also makes sense. Whereas the Q reading indicates spite toward Diomedes, the paradox of the line as it stands in F underlines the general perverseness of Thersites and the malignant and cynical pleasure he takes in unpleasant and sometimes disgusting things.

130 **that test** Q has *th' attest*, which is perhaps the better reading, but F makes good enough sense to stand.

151–4 **That cause . . . Without revolt** These knotty lines are clearer if we realize that Troilus has by this time reasoned himself into a palpable contradiction and is acutely conscious of the fact. He is saying that it is madly irrational for reason to point two ways; that would be the same as saying that reason can revolt or stop operating without being lost (perdition), or that lost reason or unreason can pass as unrevolted reason. He is virtually charging himself with sophistry in his argument that this is not Cressida.

160 **Ariachne's broken woof** The name Ariachne seems to be an amalgamation of Arachne and Ariadne, but in this context Shakespeare is clearly referring to the Arachne story. In a weaving contest with Athene, Arachne produced a magnificent piece of cloth, which Athene destroyed. Arachne thereupon hung herself, but Athene saved her by changing the rope into a spider web and Arachne into a spider.

200–1 **parrot . . . almond** Elizabethan parrots asked for almonds rather than crackers.

Act V, Scene 3

21 **For . . . much** This line appears in F as: *For we would count giue much to as violent thefts.* Tyrwhitt first suggested deleting *count* and changing *as* to *use*. This is no more than a guess, but since it is impossible to ascertain exactly what Shakespeare wrote at this point, many later editors have accepted the emendation.

27 **dear man** Many editors have replaced this *dear* with some other word, such as *brave*, *clear*, *true*. This, however, spoils Shakespeare's intentional word play on the two meanings of *dear*.

38 **lion** Lions were thought to be merciful to those that humbled themselves.

114–16 **Why . . . name** These two speeches are duplicated at the end of the play (V.10.32–4). In the Q they appear only at the end of the play. This duplication in F probably means that some sort of revision had taken place; perhaps they were written originally for this position, then shifted to the end.

Act V, Scene 4

27 Hector's match Custom allowed a high-born person to fight only with his peers.

Act V, Scene 5

6–13 Polidamus . . . Palamedes All the names in this speech are names of warriors whom Shakespeare chose at random from the earlier accounts of the Troy story in order to give an impression of feverish battle at this point. Patroclus is the only one who is a character of any importance in this play. Margarelon was a bastard son of Priam, and it may be he whom Thersites talks to at V.7.13 ff.

14 Sagittary A supernatural creature reputed to have fought for the Trojans. It was part horse, part man, and an uncommonly accurate archer.

SD Exeunt The stage direction is *Exit* in F and Q, but no previous exits have been indicated for Agamemnon or Ulysses. It is very probable that each of them left the stage after his speech, in spite of the fact that there is no indication of it in the text.

Act V, Scene 6

5 Ere that correction Ajax disputes Diomedes' right to fight Troilus since he wants to do so himself. He says if he were general he would rather give up his command than let Diomedes have the privilege of 'correcting' Troilus.

Act V, Scene 7

11 double hen'd sparrow This, the reading of F, may be wrong, but it has been allowed to stand since all the many suggested emendations are uncertain. The Q has *double hen'd Spartan*, and a most plausible suggestion has recently been made that Shakespeare originally wrote *double horn'd Spartan*.

Act V, Scene 10

7 smile Several editors have considered this a contradiction of the idea in the preceding line and have emended to *smite*. This phrase is *smile at*, not *smile on*, however, and this imputation of callous derision to the gods is in keeping with Troilus' general bitterness and cynicism at the end of the play.

46–7 painted cloths Elizabethan rooms often had mottoes and quotations worked into the tapestries or painted hangings. Pandarus is suggesting that his obscene little poem be set on the cloths of a brothel.

55 galled goose of Winchester The licensed brothels were under the jurisdiction of the Archbishop of Winchester; thus a *galled goose* was probably a prostitute with venereal disease.

56 sweat Induced sweating was used as a cure for venereal disease.

APPENDIX A

Text and Date

There are two good texts of *Troilus and Cressida*, a Quarto and the Folio, either of which could justifiably be used as the basis for a modern edition. Unusual circumstances attended the publication of each text, but, after certain shufflings on the part of the printers, in each case a text was issued which has a certain degree of authority.

The history of the Quarto starts with an entry in the Stationers' Register for February 7, 1603: 'Master Roberts. Entered for his copie in full Court holden this day to print when he hath gotten sufficient aucthority for yt, The booke of Troilus and Cresseda, as yt is acted by my lord Chamberlens Men.' This license probably refers to Shakespeare's play, but it was evidently not acted upon, for no *Troilus and Cressida* came out at this time. Six years later, however, another entry was made in the Stationers' Register licensing the publishers Bonian and Walley to print a play called *The History of Troylus and Cressida*, which had been acted by Shakespeare's company. Soon after this entry of January 1609, possibly in the spring, the Quarto appeared.

There are two variant states of this 1609 Quarto. The first has a title page which reads: 'THE / Historie of Troylus / and Cresseida./ As it was acted by the Kings Maiesties / servants at the Globe. / Written by William Shakespeare. / [Design] / LONDON / Imprinted by G. Eld for R. Bonian and H. Walley, and / are to be sold at the spred Eagle in Paules / Church-yeard, over against the / great North doore. / 1609.' While the printing of this issue was going forward, for some unknown reason the printer stopped printing, canceled the title page, reset the type of the upper half of it, and added a prefatory epistle before the text.[1] Some of the extant copies of Q have the earlier title page, and

---

1. This Epistle is printed as Appendix C on page 168 of this edition.

some the later,[2] but it is clear that for the body of the text all the copies are from one single edition and were printed from the same forms. The new title page and the Epistle raise several problems which have never been completely solved, in that they imply that the play had not been acted, despite the statements of the first title page and the Stationers' Register that it had. This claim that the play had never been 'clapper-claw'd with the palms of the vulgar' may or may not be true, since the Epistle is patently an advertising blurb designed to increase sales among the would-be wits. In any case, it can safely be said that the play was not particularly popular; no performance of it is recorded elsewhere, and it was not printed again until the publication of the Folio in 1623.

In the First Folio *Troilus and Cressida* was originally scheduled to follow *Romeo and Juliet* in the section of the book containing the tragedies. Three pages of type had already been set up when the printer stopped work, probably because of difficulties with the copyright, and the play was eventually printed between the histories and the tragedies, after *Henry VIII* and before *Coriolanus*. In this new position there was added a prologue which does not appear in Q.

Several theories have been put forward to explain these curious changes in F, as there have been to explain the changes in Q, but in both cases the explanations offered often do not get far out of the realm of theory and into the area of fact. A recent series of articles,[3] however, has established with clear proof the

2. By some sort of slip on the part of the binder, the Yale Elizabethan Club copy contains both title pages and the Epistle.

3. Peter Alexander, *"Troilus and Cressida*, 1609," *The Library*, 4th ser., *9* (1928), 265–86; Philip Williams, "Shakespeare's *Troilus and Cressida:* The Relationship of the Quarto and the Folio," *Studies in Bibliography, 3* (University of Virginia, 1950), 131–43; Alice Walker, "The Textual Problem of *Troilus and Cressida,*" *Modern Language Review, 45* (1950), 459–64; W. W. Greg, "The Printing of Shakespeare's *Troilus and Cressida* in the First Folio," *Papers of the Bibliographical Society of America, 45* (1951), 273–82; Alice Walker, *Textual Problems of the First Folio* (Cambridge, England, 1953).

relationship between the text of the Folio and the text of the Quarto. The first three pages in F were set up in type directly from a copy of Q. After the resumption of printing, with *Troilus* in its new location, the 'copy' used was a copy of Q which had been collated with an independently authoritative manuscript, whether a promptbook or foul papers. A good many changes were made in the Q text during the collation, including some which correct printer's errors and some which introduce completely new readings. F prefaces the play with a prologue which does not exist in Q, and in addition augments the text with some forty-odd new lines scattered throughout the play, most of which are unmistakably genuine. Even the prologue, poor as it is as poetry, cannot be proved to be by another hand. Thus, in a sense, F is a derivative text, but at the same time it is often more authoritative than the text it was derived from. For this reason, the present edition follows the Folio text as closely as possible. If Q had been used, it would have been necessary to make a conflate text by adding lines from F; and certainly if F's changes have any authority at all, either from the author or the playhouse, it cannot be said that Q is the sole substantive text. When it has been advisable to use the Q reading for individual words, F's reading is given in the glosses: for example, I.1.22 **leavening** F *leau'ing*. When neither the F nor Q reading is satisfactory, the text has been emended. This has occurred only when it was absolutely necessary, and the emendations are printed in square brackets and explained in the notes. Any added stage directions which do not appear in F are also printed in square brackets. Punctuation has been kept as close as practicable to that of F and Q, but in many cases it has been changed to conform with modern practice. In accordance with the general policy of this series, spellings which indicate Renaissance pronunciation have been retained, although the Folio's inconsistencies in spelling of words like *nere*, *ne're*, *ene*, *e'ne*, when they indicate nothing about pronunciation, have been reduced to consistency.

Dating the composition of the play with any exactitude is virtually impossible. If we take the 1603 entry in the Stationers' Register to refer to Shakespeare's play, as most scholars are willing to do, we at least have a *terminus ad quem* for its composition. It is not included in Francis Meres' list of Shakespeare's plays in *Palladis Tamia* in 1598,[4] so we can take that date as the earlier limit. To narrow the date down further, a great many ingenious arguments have been offered of varying credibility, most of them depending on alleged topical allusions in the play. This play has long been associated with the so-called War of the Theaters, and although many scholars do not accept the identification of certain characters in this play with certain of Shakespeare's contemporaries, there remains the suspicion that this play has some connection with Ben Jonson's *Poetaster*, which was produced in 1601. The amount of connection is in dispute, and many of the topical allusions are doubtful. Even though such vagueness is unsatisfactory, it is probably unwise to date the play more precisely than 'shortly before 1603.'

4. Leslie Hotson's contention in his *Shakespeare's Sonnets Dated* (London, 1949) that this play is the puzzling *Loves Labours Wonne* of Meres' list is not at all convincing.

162

APPENDIX B
Sources

Troilus and Cressida is one of the most difficult of Shakespeare's plays to deal with in regard to its sources. We know in general where he could have gotten his Troy material, but we lack conclusive proofs to demonstrate the immediate origin of the play.

This play is, of course, a composite work, combining two threads of action, the Troilus-Cressida love story and the military plot involving the larger struggle between the Greeks and the Trojans. The Troilus portion is easier to deal with, since its main source lies in Chaucer's great poem, *Troilus and Criseyde*. The story had had a complicated earlier history, and in spite of claims that it was originally a classical story, it was really the invention of medieval writers. Although several of the personages in the story appear in Homer's *Iliad*, they are there little more than names, and the love narrative did not appear in any recognizable form until it was written in the *Roman de Troie* by Benoit de Sainte-Maure, a French poet of the 12th century. It was copied with few changes into the *Historia Trojana*, a 13th-century Latin prose work by Guido delle Colonne. The story was extracted from the mass of Trojan history in which it was embedded by Boccaccio, whose *Filostrato* expands the story and treats it as a center of focus for an artistic unity. Chaucer, in writing his version, followed Boccaccio's poem, but expanded it and developed the characterizations until it became what is probably the only unquestioned masterpiece dealing with this story.

A comparison of Shakespeare's play with Chaucer's poem reveals many points in which Shakespeare was following the plot outline of Chaucer, but it at the same time makes us conscious of a wide difference in tone and attitude toward the various characters. Shakespeare has sometimes been accused of debasing Chaucer's characters, as he has been accused of debasing the Homeric characters in the military plot. The characters had been considerably degraded, however, before they came to Shakespeare. The edition of Chaucer's works printed by Thynne in 1532 included a poem by the 15th-century Scots poet, Robert

Henryson, entitled *The Testament of Cressid.* This poem continues the Cressida story and reduces her to a beggar and a leper before her death. Throughout the 16th century Henryson's poem was thought to be part of Chaucer's work, in spite of the fact that it is written in the lowland dialect of Scotland, and the just punishment of the heroine evidently appealed to many readers. There are a very great number of treatments of the story during the 16th century, ranging from a Latin play by Nicholas Grimald, through lyrics, songs, and broadside ballads, to mere chance references in similes and metaphors. By Shakespeare's time the story had become common property of the people, known undoubtedly to many who had never read Chaucer or Henryson. Pandarus was taken as the type for the pimp or go-between, and such was his fame that before the middle of the century *pander* had become a common noun. Cressida was so well established in the popular mind as a loose, unfaithful woman that the phrase 'a woman of Cressid's kind,' meaning a whore, had become a cliché.[1] Thus Shakespeare's characterizations of these people represent not so much his reinterpretation of the story as his acceptance of the tradition as it came down to him.

The same thing is true of his treatment of the personages in the military plot. Throughout the Middle Ages and on into the Renaissance, the Troy story was almost always told with sympathy for the Trojans, and several Western nations fancifully traced their origins to some colonizing Trojan hero who wandered as a displaced person after the war. Homer in the original was little known in England until the 16th century, and the derogatory medieval conception of Greek characters like Achilles, Ajax, and Agamemnon continued even after some Englishmen had begun reading Homer. The two earlier authorities whom Shake-

1. The change in conception of the Troilus story during the 16th century is treated in full by Hyder Rollins, 'The Troilus-Cressida Story from Chaucer to Shakespeare,' *PMLA*, *32* (1917), 383–429. Some few facts are added to this body of information by W. B. D. Henderson, 'Shakespeare's *Troilus and Cressida* Yet Deeper in its Tradition,' *The Parrott Presentation Volume* (Princeton, 1935), pp. 127–56.

speare seems to have used were Lydgate's *Troy Book* and Caxton's *Recuyell of the Historyes of Troye*. Lydgate's poem is a compendium of virtually all the stories connected with Troy, drawn principally from Guido delle Colonne's *Historia Trojana*. Caxton's *Recuyell* is a translation of *Le Recueil de Troyennes Ystoires* by a French prose writer, Raoul le Fevre. Details of plot incident from Shakespeare's play have been traced to each of these sources,[2] but it must be admitted that few really convincing verbal parallels have been cited. Any material Shakespeare got from them had been pretty thoroughly assimilated by the time it reissued from his pen, for his dependence on them is not nearly so obvious as was his use of his sources for the English history plays or the Gloucester plot of *Lear*.

Shakespeare probably made use also of George Chapman's famous translation of Homer, although at the time this play appears to have been written only eight books of the translation had been printed. Books I, II, VII through XI, and XVIII, which were issued in 1598, do include a brief characterization of Thersites, who is completely missing in Caxton and Lydgate.[3] Again in this case, however, it must be stated that no truly inescapable cases of verbal parallelism have been discovered, and we can by no means ignore the possibility that Shakespeare might have read his Homer, or parts of it, in a Latin translation or even in the Greek.

As always in considering Shakespeare's sources, we have the picture of his using diverse materials, in this case Chaucer, Lydgate, Caxton, Homer, and probably a certain amount of popular, bookless tradition; but his combination of those materials into a unified, two-plot play, written at least in part in language which compares favorably with his greatest, is a unique achievement. There have been serious critical doubts about his complete success in the over-all structure and tone of the play, but few critics

2. One or two minor items have been traced to Robert Greene's *Euphues His Censure to Philautus*, published in 1587.

3. Recently Robert Presson has argued that Shakespeare followed Chapman in many basic details, and followed Lydgate very little.

have denied that it contains many magnificently conceived scenes and speeches.

Before leaving the subject, some mention should be made of the theory that there was an earlier Troilus play which Shakespeare used as his source. As is the case with *Hamlet,* there is not now in existence any play which Shakespeare might have revised to become the play we have, but many scholars have long suspected that there was once such a play. We have record of several 16th-century plays on the Troy theme, two of which are mentioned in Henslowe's diary at the end of the century. *Troy* was performed in 1596, and a play was being written by Dekker and Chettle on the subject in 1599. Since these have not survived,[4] we can never be sure just how much influence they had on Shakespeare's play. He probably drew little from them directly, since they belonged to a rival company, but considering the obvious popularity of this material there is the bare possibility that still other Troy plays were available to him. A play by Thomas Heywood called *The Iron Age* treats most of the events covered by Shakespeare and shows some striking similarities to *Troilus;* but it was very probably written after Shakespeare's play, unless, as has been conjectured, the *Troy* mentioned by Henslowe is an earlier version of *Iron Age.*[5] Many readers have criticized the treatment Shakespeare gives to the conclusion of his play, and some have surmised that in his revision of some earlier play, he lost interest for some reason toward the end and gave the battle scenes in the last act very few of his master touches. Although this may be true, it is a mistake to argue that the scenes are not Shakespeare's simply because no great poetry appears. A large-scale battle scene such as that which runs from V.4 to V.9 was a rapid paced spectacle of movement and action,

4. A 'plot' or sketch of entrances and exits for some Troilus play has survived. It is generally thought that it belongs to the lost play of Dekker and Chettle.

5. This play and the other Elizabethan works dealing with the Troy story are studied by J. S. P. Tatlock, 'The Siege of Troy in Elizabethan Literature, Especially in Shakespeare and Heywood,' *PMLA, 30* (1915), 673–770.

and the sketchy verbal scenario supplied for it is quite adequate to allow stirring production effects. The theory of Shakespeare's revision of any earlier play, which in turn, presumably, drew from Chaucer, Lydgate, and Caxton, must remain merely a plausible possibility until such a play is discovered.

A Never Writer, to an Ever Reader. News.

Eternal reader, you have here a new play, never stal'd with the Stage, never clapper-claw'd with the palms of the vulgar, and yet passing full of the palm comical, for it is a birth of your brain that never undertook anything comical vainly. And were but the vain names of comedies changed for the titles of commodities, or of plays for pleas, you should see all those grand censors, that now style them such vanities, flock to them for the main grace of their gravities, especially this author's comedies, that are so fram'd to the life that they serve for the most common commentaries of all the actions of our lives, showing such a dexterity and power of wit that the most displeased with plays are pleas'd with his comedies. And all such dull and heavy-witted worldlings as were never capable of the wit of a comedy, coming by report of them to his representations, have found that wit there that they never found in themselves and have parted better witted than they came, feeling an edge of wit set upon them more than ever they dreamed they had brain to grind it on. So much and such savored salt of wit is in his comedies that they seem, for their height of pleasure, to be born in that sea that brought forth Venus. Amongst all there is none more witty than this; and had I time I would comment upon it, though I know it needs not, for so much as will make you think your testern well bestowed, but for so much worth as even poor I know to be stuff'd in it. It deserves such a labour as well as the best comedy in Terence or Plautus. And believe this, that when he is gone and his comedies out of sale, you will scramble for them and set up a new English Inquisition. Take this for a warning, and at the peril of your pleasure's loss and judgment's, refuse not nor like this the less for not being sullied with the smoky breath of the multitude, but thank fortune for the scape it hath made amongst you, since by the grand possessors' wills I believe you should have pray'd for them rather than been pray'd. And so I leave all such to be pray'd for, for the state of their wits' healths, that will not praise it. Vale.[1]

1. This epistle appeared in the second issue of the Quarto of *Troilus and Cressida*.

APPENDIX D
Reading List

A New Variorium of Shakespeare: *Troilus and Cressida,* ed. by H. Hillebrand, supplemental ed. T. W. Baldwin. Philadelphia, 1953.

C. F. TUCKER BROOKE, 'Shakespeare's Study in Culture and Anarchy,' *Yale Review, 17,* 571–7.

G. WILSON KNIGHT, 'The Philosophy of *Troilus and Cressida,*' *The Wheel of Fire,* London, 1930.

W. W. LAWRENCE, *Shakespeare's Problem Comedies,* New York, 1931.

HYDER ROLLINS, 'The Troilus-Cressida Story from Chaucer to Shakespeare,' *PMLA, 32,* 383–429.

THEODORE SPENCER, 'A Commentary on Shakespeare's *Troilus and Cressida,*' *Tokyo Studies in English Literature, 16,* 1–43.

E. M. W. TILLYARD, *Shakespeare's Problem Plays,* Toronto, 1949.